GO FISHING
with
John Wilson

GO FISHING
with
John Wilson

ANGLIA
Television Limited

BOXTREE

DEDICATION

This book is for Peter Akehurst without whose single-minded endeavours our 'Go Fishing' programmes would never have been made.

And for Tony Morgan who first took me roach fishing when I wanted merely to buy some goldfish.

First published in Great Britain in 1989
by Boxtree Limited

Reprinted 1989 and 1990
First published in paperback 1991

This edition published for Books UK 1994

Go Fishing copyright © Anglia Television 1989
Photographs copyright © by Anglia Television 1989
(pages 1, 9, 53, 61, 79, 97, 104)
Text copyright and all other photographs copyright © John Wilson 1989

A catalogue entry for this title is available from the British Library

Line drawings by Raymond Turvey

Typeset by Bookworm Typesetting in Manchester

Printed and bound in Italy by New Interlitho S.p.A.
for Boxtree Limited, Broadwall House,
21 Broadwall, London SE1 9PL

Contents

Introduction

Getting away from it all is what most of us like about fishing, and much of the pleasure comes from being alone in beautiful surroundings. However, the location provides more than just a picturesque backdrop; it also creates the other ingredient essential to the fisherman's enjoyment, the challenge. It is for this reason that I have deliberately divided the book into locations, rather than employ the more conventional format of a chapter for each species of fish. The emphasis is on observation, stealth, watercraft and opportunism. Patience and impatience, too, play a large part in my approach.

What this book is not is a comprehensive guide to technique. Instead I have been deliberately selective, covering those methods which I prefer to use and the places where I have most enjoyed putting them into action. Whilst my methods may not be the only methods, I hope that even the beginner will find here sufficient technique to meet the challenge of the waters, wherever he fishes.

John Wilson
Great Witchingham
August 1988

About the Author

Acclaimed by anglers across the country as the best fishing programmes ever shown on the television, 'Go Fishing', presented by Norfolk angler John Wilson, has three series under its belt with more on the drawing board for independent nationwide viewing.

Born in Enfield, North London in 1943, John Wison's introduction to the mystery of fishing came as a five-year-old when taken to the local brook by his father to net for sticklebacks and stone loach; and he has been fascinated by water and the fish in it ever since. John caught his first carp, a 3–lb wildie from the local squire's lakes during the early hours before starting his paper round; and at the age of thirteen he attended an inaugural meeting of what was to become the Enfield Town Angling Society, which is still going strong after thirty years. The club's formation stimulated John's interest in travelling further afield from his local River Lea. He fished many of the major rivers in southern England, extending to those of Norfolk and Suffolk after buying his first motor bike.

By profession a ladies' hairdresser, and having also spent a couple of years in lithographic printing, John joined the Merchant Navy in his early twenties for what was to be a three-year voyage on P & O lines SS *Oronsay*, fishing in over fifty countries from Bermuda to Japan. Laden with tackle, he would usually be first ashore when the ship docked. His most memorable fish was actually lost whilst the ship made way to leave port in Auckland harbour, New Zealand. It was a gigantic stingray estimated at over 500 lbs, which parted company after a two-hour fight when a crewman of the tug alongside the *Oronsay* tried to heave it aboard. Fishing from the ship, 30 ft above the waterline, proved a real problem, which John eventually solved by constructing an equally large drop net. In this, many rays and sharks to 8 ft long found their way up the side of the ship and eventually on board.

At the age of twenty-five John left the *Oronsay* to get married and flew off with his wife, Barbara, to Barbados in the West Indies, where they managed a chain of hairdressing salons for three years. Once again, John was soon exploring the local fishing potential. Apart from crewing on a big game fishing boat on his day off, he searched for high-jumping tarpon among the swamps during his lunch breaks and from the beach at night, where he landed tarpon to nearly 100 lbs and stingrays to over 200 lbs.

With their wooden cottage perched on the rocks only a stone's throw from the sea, John also developed a love for skin-diving and spent at

opposite No wonder it takes up to three days to put just one half hour programme together. How would you like producing the goods to order with this lot wading in the lake? Director/ Producer Peter Akehurst looks on painfully, waiting for the photographer to finish.

least a couple of hours each day spear-fishing and exploring the many reefs among the clear blue waters of the west coast.

After three years the Wilsons returned home to Norfolk where John had enjoyed fishing in his late teens. At this point the Wilsons sank all their savings into a fishing tackle shop in Norwich; and this is where John has been serving and giving advice to the anglers of Norwich since 1971.

John occasionally scuba-dives local fisheries and writes regularly for British and foreign angling journals, he also contributes to books. His local guide *Where to Fish in Norfolk and Suffolk* enjoys its third update and reprint since first being published in 1973.

Complementing John's writing, photography has been an important hobby for over twenty years and he specialises in colour transparencies.

John lives with Barbara, teenage children Lee and Lisa, and a horde of pets on the outskirts of Norwich in a lakeland setting, where in his spare time he enjoys putting his experience into fisheries management.

1
'Go Fishing'
The Beginning

Go Fishing

Although I have been a keen still-life angling photographer for more years than I care to remember, my introduction to televised fishing occurred through the sheer persistence of producer/director Peter Akehurst. Peter had long nursed a burning ambition to make a good fishing programme and asked me to help put some pilot videos together. With a freelance crew, we filmed roach fishing on a tiny stream, chub on the River Wensum and pike fishing on the Norfolk Broads.

We approached the various television companies and almost three years later Peter's determination paid off when Anglia Television engaged our services to make a series of six programmes. 'Go Fishing' was born.

From the moment of that first pilot programme Peter and I began to recognise the innumerable problems associated with the televising of fishing. In the case of other sports or pastimes – a snooker contest, a boxing match, a swimming gala or an athletics meeting – the action is predictable and occurs within a fixed, prearranged time slot. Even a goalless football game can be enjoyed by the viewer. Not so with fishing. Indeed, we have sometimes wondered whether viewers would accept a fishing programme without a fish being caught. Let's hope we never have to find out.

We do have the advantage, however, of a wide variety of interesting and colourful settings. In researching each programme I aim to find beautiful, enchanting spots which not only look inviting on the screen but also offer a choice of camera angles. As a rule these are fairly secluded, for trying to film fishing is difficult enough without having to contend with folk who, at the sight of a television camera, are drawn like bees to a honey pot. Those programmes we have filmed on day ticket waters, and even free fisheries, have created the worst problems. People have to be asked to move away from the camera, or to vacate the spot where they are fishing, so that the shots synchronise with those of yesterday when the banks were bare; and sometimes you just can't win.

It is the element of chance which makes the sport of fishing so frustratingly difficult to capture on camera. Unlike a 90–minute football match, the cameras cannot be running continually during a three-day shoot, which is about the time it takes to put a 'Go Fishing' episode together. And even if they were, there is no guarantee that a particular high note, like the biggest fish of the day, will be filmed. All sorts of things conspire to ensure the very opposite, such as running out of tape, batteries going flat, a low-flying jet zooming overhead to drown the soundtrack, or the cameraman happening to be panning around doing a fill-in shot just as the fish is being hooked. Add to this the inconsistency of our British weather and you have an idea of some of our problems.

'Go Fishing': The beginning

What goes up must come down. This was proved by the pike which refused to be held for the camera and which shattered John's carbon rod just below the spigot, before escaping back into Ardleigh Reservoir near Colchester. A favourite clip among 'Go Fishing' viewers. Not a favourite of John's!

No matter what the weather conditions, it is particularly difficult to convey the enjoyment of catching relatively small fish, which, even to keen anglers, rarely look exciting on the television screen. Anyone can relate to the awesome jaws of a big shark or the spectacular acrobatics of a marlin or a sailfish in a colourful, tropical setting. Given palm trees, sundrenched beaches, and blue clear water, even a chocolate bar advert can hold the viewer's attention. Filming on a wet, windy, overcast day, beneath a line of oaks, hardly exercises the same appeal. So we always pray for sunlight and for the result it brings to colour television. Everything from the subtle colours of marginal plants and wild flowers to the mosaic spotting of a pike's body looks far more alive and stunning if bathed in natural sunlight.

Fortunately, fishing is not only about catching fish. Contrary to the belief of the minority groups who knock our sport, most anglers are lovers of the countryside and its wildlife. We all derive enormous enjoyment from the surroundings in which we fish, otherwise why would we do it? The birds, mammals, insects and amphibians, the wild flowers and trees, the misty dawns and colourful sunsets, are as much a part of our day as the fishing itself.

So when we make 'Go Fishing', we also deliberately highlight those things that the angler and most nature lovers see, but do not necessarily relate to individually because it is all part of a day out on the water. Through presenting these programmes I have rekindled my childhood love of waterside plants and wild flowers. There is so much to learn about their shape, smell, colour, growth and reproductive processes.

3

John Wilson's eye view. It's rather off-putting isn't it?

opposite What the viewer never sees are the camera crews which cover John's every move. Here on the Hampshire Avon the usually secluded swim has been invaded on both banks.

Programme content is thus to a large extent dictated by the walk which Peter and I try to take an evening or two before each shoot. Always there is something to catch the attention, perhaps a particular plant or creature we all take for granted, so it is nice to record its presence and the pleasure it gives.

Our first series of 'Go Fishing', featuring six 'species' programmes – pike, trout, chub, roach, tench and carp – was a unique step for Anglia Television. They were in fact the very first documentary programmes produced on the then new, compact Betacam video system, both in camerawork and editing terms. Totally integrated and extremely compact, the Betacam uses standard half-inch tape and includes a Canon 14–1 zoom lens which doubles to a 28–1 image.

My invisible connection to no. 1 camera is via a cordless radio mike. Viewers tend to spot the tiniest details yet no one ever appears to be looking for the clip-on mike which is always on my jacket lapel, the battery pack being situated in an inside pocket. I become completely unaware of its presence and can easily natter on, uninhibited

throughout the three-day shoot. What does put me under enormous pressure, however relaxed I may seem, is trying to catch fish literally to order. Despite relishing the challenge and the buzz from it all, I always feel relieved when it's finally 'all in the can', and we wrap.

Being completely self-contained, the Betacam system is very portable and can be worked with a minimal field team. Our crew consists of two cameramen, sound recordist, electrician, director/producer and his assistant, plus myself. There are no make-up artists or canteen facilities. Just seven people intent on putting together the fun of fishing, sometimes in the rain, sometimes in the mud and often crouched in awkward locations. Mind you, that's still six more pairs of feet around than I would normally choose to be fishing with, but the Betacam system does allow for maximum flexibility. For instance, compared to film, because it works on electrical impulses the Betacam system can reproduce colour in much lower light conditions. Watching some playbacks on the monitor during one particularly overcast day, I couldn't believe it was the same place I was actually fishing.

Just as well really, for we suffer enough waiting for the sun to come out to preserve continuity after the start of a sequence shot in sunlight. As a stills photographer I had never envisaged how long and drawn out the process of making movie films can be. There are so many takes to cram into what is often a very short period while the light holds and there are fish to catch. 'Do you think you'll get a bite this cast, John?' is a favourite director's question. I ask you!

No matter how well you plan, there is always the unexpected, like the severe flooding during the summer and autumn of 1987 which turned my planned shoot, the lovely Little Ouse running through Barnham near Thetford, into a raging torrent several hundred yards wide within a few days. A lot of research had gone into Series Two and this particular programme, with the help of the late Bill Clarke, whose catches of pound-plus dace from the river were legendary. Despite health problems, Bill generously provided a tour of all his favourite haunts.

August could not come round quick enough and two weeks before the shoot I popped over to the river for a look. There were big dace everywhere and conditions looked perfect. The only problem was the old bridge over a deep dyke where all the camera and sound equipment would have to be carried. I decided that it simply had to be rebuilt and so my wife, Barbara, and I spent most of the following Sunday doing just that. The long 6 x 10 inch cross timbers were OK but all the slats were completely rotten. After being stung to bits by the tall nettles which had to be beaten down for working access, we got stuck in, actually finishing the task by late afternoon. Little did I realise at the time that it was now a bridge miles from nowhere which would never be used.

Only two days later the whole of Norfolk was about to suffer the worst summer flooding in living memory. By the weekend rivers everywhere were brown, completely over the banks and quite unfishable. Our 'little river' shoot was impossible. But the film crew had been booked months earlier for the shoot and had to be charged against our programme budget. I was forced to do some pretty quick thinking indeed.

Fortunately, the problem was instantly solved as I drowned my sorrows in the local with a friend who happened to be the River Wensum mill owner. Out of the blue, Geoff remarked, 'It's a pity you didn't do a programme over in my mill pool, John.' His words were like pennies from heaven. I had, in fact, considered the idea but didn't want to ask in case he encountered undesirable after-effects (such as 'Can I fish your pool?') once the programme had been on the box. Geoff, however, was quite unconcerned and welcomed my proposals. Plan B was now put into action. Although the river above the mill and the weir pool were out, a nice piece of slack water existed immediately outside the mill house where the gates are rarely opened.

Here at least was somewhere to fish in a river, and so I changed the programme to 'Weir Pool Magic'; and magic it certainly was. Amongst a whole bunch of big fish I fluked out a brace of Wensum roach, together weighing over 5 lbs, actually while the cameras were rolling.

Unfortunately there was a sad end to this my favourite programme of all. When we switched venues from the unfishable Little Ouse to the Wensum, I rang old Bill Clarke several times but there was no reply. A week after the shoot I rang again and Bill's wife answered the phone. 'Oh, John, didn't you know,' she said, 'Bill passed away on the 15th, the very day you were going to film on the river.' For once in my life words were very difficult to find.

Another quick switch and change of plan occurred just two months later when the phone rang at 9.30 pm on Sunday 1 November, only one day before the shoot on a lovely secluded mere in deepest Suffolk. Without any apparent reason, the man who controlled fishing on the Mere (let's call him Mr X – although I used a different term at the time) decided he wouldn't allow the programme to be filmed there after all.

I tried to prick his conscience with the 'soft' approach, just managing

Capturing the nature angle in 'Weir Pool Magic', John's favourite of all the 'Go Fishing' programmes. Eels however do not oblige on cue.

not to lose my temper but Mr X wasn't having any. So I rang Peter Akehurst with the good news and he too tried to reason with the man. Peter, however, went over the edge and was promptly told what to do. 'What now?' asked Peter. 'The cameras and crew are all booked for Tuesday morning. We have got to film somewhere.'

I rang off, promising to come up with a location, though it's a near impossible task to organise something, which usually takes several months of careful research, within twenty-four hours. My boat was already fitted up with swivel chair, sonar equipment and other American-style gizmos for the mere and its big perch and pike, so I was really looking for a similar venue that would allow me to boat fish using artificial lures.

After a few minutes of panic followed by an hour of vacant thoughts, the name 'Ardleigh Reservoir' in Essex suddenly came to mind. I had not actually fished there or even seen the water but had planned to at a future date, so all the information was in my telephone book. It was now 10.15 pm on a Sunday evening; surely Richard Connell, the fishery manager, would never be in his office at such a late hour. But luckily he was catching up on some bookwork and about to head off home when the phone rang. I blurted out a potted version of the dilemma and immediately Richard invited us to Ardleigh to try to put a programme together. That's what I call service and I shall be forever grateful to him.

Richard even offered us the flat-bottomed handicapped angler's boat with a flap-down end – and what a boon that turned out to be with the first camera crew. Keeping the camera level when out afloat is always a headache. We located a nice piece of sloping shoreline where I could slip my custom built boat off the trailer for the introduction to the programme, and within 48 hours of being let down we were actually out afloat on a completely new venue.

One of the headaches I face as presenter of the 'Go Fishing' programmes is that I have absolutely no way of telling what piece of action the editor will use in the final cut. On a three-day shoot, with ten to twelve hours of fishing each day on tape, reducing it all into just twenty-six minutes is indeed a problem. Much of what I might consider to be perfectly usable material has to be omitted due to the time slot. But obviously you can't include everything, for there's much more to each programme than just showing fish being caught one after another.

Sometimes we make dreadful mistakes whilst filming. As on the morning of our third and last day at Ardleigh, when a series of silly but quite spontaneous cock-ups actually caused me to lose my bottle and swear on camera, something I consciously try to avoid at all costs. But this really was the last straw.

It was bad enough that Peter told the crew to wrap just after lunch

Despite all the electrical wizardry . . . . look at the size of this perch. Note John's high swivel chair, a real boon for working lures in comfort.

when I had been promised a two clear hours continuous fishing on camera, presenting static dead baits on both rods in the hope of a big pike. It was even worse when everyone except me rowed over to dry land for drinks! Determined to show them that there was one pro in the team, I decided to hang it out.

Although there had been plenty of interest, with mainly small fish, up to this time, I felt the programme really needed the lift of a good fish as a finale. Besides, for the first time in three days the sun was actually about to poke its head through the blanket of grey, and when that happens in deep water the increased light values down there close to the bottom in 25 feet of water is like a 'dinner gong' to lethargic predators. I suddenly felt very confident indeed – any minute I thought, I'll show 'em.

Lunch was now over and Peter yelled out, 'Come on John, wrap it!' Sue and Chris were in fact coming across for my radio mike, as they all prepared to row back, dismantling gear as they went. At that precise second, line plinked from the rubber band on the handle above the reel and slowly started to peel from the spool.

My announcement of 'I've got a run on a dead bait, quick turn over' acted like a time bomb. Talk about move fast – there were plugs, sockets and mikes going in all directions as the two camera crews rowed back into position. But it was all too late for me. There was no way I wanted a deeply hooked pike, so I struck instantly and enjoyed the powerful scrap of a good fish in deep water, while seething beneath my

9

opposite The reward of a rich estate lake. A beautiful 6½lb tench caught close-in just beyond the marginal edges on breadflake presented beneath a simple lift method float rig.

breath in the knowledge that only the end of the fight would be filmed. They were only ready and fired up to go, in fact, just before the fish made its last roll and I brought it alongside the boat for handing out. They had missed a really exciting fight – powerful dives, tail walking, plus a 'once round the boat' run that I was powerless to stop. I could gladly have throttled Peter and it was probably just as well he wasn't in the same boat. Naturally I tried not to allow my anger and frustration show, talking viewers through the chain of events as usual, remarking how the pike, a beautifully conditioned plump fish of around 14 lbs, had a peculiar lump on its back.

Then it happened. The moment which, of all our eighteen programmes, viewers seem to remember best. The pike decided to do a reverse twist, backward, jack knife somersault over my right shoulder (which was bad enough) but then proceeded to hit my carbon pike rod on its way back into the reservoir, breaking it several inches below the spigot. Well, that was it for me. I was livid. In fact, how I managed to confine myself to 'Well, that takes the bloody biscuit!' remains an utter mystery. I could have turned the Essex air purple.

It all seems terribly important at the time, although what we are really talking about is just an extra half hour of television! Put into perspective, our problems are, I guess, laughable. But it's difficult to be anything other than professional, and there are many occasions when I have felt like screaming both on and off camera.

One of the most desperate situations was having all my carefully prepared tackle nicked from the car by a drunk, an hour before I set off to make the roach programme in Series One. By an amazing coincidence I happened to drive past the guy staggering along with the bundle under his arm on the way to his local secondhand shop, and retrieved the lot. I immediately headed for our destination of Homersfield, a beautifully mature lake owned by my good friend Norman Symonds. Generously, Norman had given us a complete run of the place but he had no control over the elements; overnight frosts at the beginning of September, so hard that it put down the roach I was after. Not that it mattered, because Peter was not satisfied with the introductions until after lunch – when the camera decided to pack up.

Twenty-four hours in the life of a TV angling programme presenter. All his tackle stolen, worst September frosts for fifty years, camera packing up – day one over. In theory one-third of our programme already in the bag; in reality a twenty-nine-second clip of me staggering down the steep banking cluttered with gear and picking a blackberry. And people say to me, 'No wonder you catch fish on your programmes, John, anyone would in three days!'

Which is perfectly true – but try filming it!

2
Estate Lakes
Fishing for Tench

Go Fishing

The very first episode of *Go Fishing* was filmed, appropriately enough, amidst the beautiful and tranquil setting of a Norfolk estate lake. When we began filming I was dressed in a sweat shirt and corduroy waistcoat; for continuity's sake I had to stay wearing this outfit throughout the shoot during what turned out to be the hottest three days of 1986.

Estate lakes are my favourite still waters and are without question among the most picturesque fisheries in this country. Just about every county has man-made lakes dug during the eighteenth and nineteenth centuries to enhance the estates of rich landowners. Landscaping and lake design on a grand scale were undertaken by architects of outstanding talent such as Capability Brown, who incidentally was responsible for many of the estate lakes where I now fish in Norfolk and Suffolk. For the rich it was fashionable and thus desirable to have a valley or stream dammed to create an ornamental lake. The dam would be constructed of brick, with a sluice for the stream to escape. The lake would always be within the sight of the great hall, affording spectacular views; and summer houses of ornate design, diving platforms and boat houses were built for leisure activities. Thus it is with very few exceptions that all estate lakes follow a similar pattern. They start shallow, sometimes mere inches deep, and quite narrow at the point where the stream from high ground enters, and meander through the valley, finishing at their deepest and widest next to the dam wall.

Many of the older estate lakes have actually long since ceased to exist as fertile fisheries. They have simply silted up with sediment brought in by the feeding stream or with leaf fall from the trees, great oaks, beech, maple and willow which preside over their banks; often both are contributory factors. Eventually the land reclaims its own, a fact of life with all man-made fisheries, which actually start dying (in depth that is) from the moment they are constructed. To arrest this perfectly natural evolutionary process, many great lakes are periodically dredged. Nowadays, surface suction pumps can return the lake to its original form in a matter of weeks by drawing up the vast layers of silt accumulated over the decades, through a large-diameter pipe. This silt is often spread over farmland as a rich organic fertiliser. A century ago it was a case of all the villagers turning out with bucket and spade in return for a good lunch. Most fishing clubs today would be more than pleased if a quarter of the members turned up to join working parties during the close season!

Estate lakes are primarily for the summer angler, though winter sport with pike, perch and even rudd can prove hectic in spells of mild weather, particularly when coupled with a warm south-westerly air stream. But to me, these creations of our forefathers signify one species above all others – tench; and almost always of a high average size.

The secret lies, literally, within the rich organic layer of silt covering the bottom of the lake, sometimes 2–4 ft thick. This is an incredibly abundant source of natural food. When you see great clusters of bubbles on the surface during the summer months in the early morning, you can be sure the tench are rooting about for bloodworms, the bright red aquatic larvae of the midge fly. It is a feeding spree which can sometimes last well into the day, and on rare occasions all day long. Binoculars are invaluable for locating these areas where tench feed naturally. Their tiny bubbles are difficult to see with the naked eye over distances of 40 yards unless the sun is catching them. It is worth spending as much time as possible in reconnaissance, perhaps even more time than you eventually spend fishing, because if the fish aren't there, you can't catch them.

Tench also feed on shrimps, water boatmen, *Asellus* crustaceans and tiny pea mussels, as well as the huge meandering clouds of zoo-plankton of which the largest and best known is the daphnia or water flea. These creatures make up a large proportion of the diet of tench during the warmest months, and when tench are hard on daphnia they are frustratingly difficult to tempt with conventional baits. Midsummer reservoir trout anglers experience a similar phenomenon with rainbow

A typical Norfolk Estate lake, purpose built at the foot of a valley to be overlooked by the great hall. Quite simply a tench fisher's paradise.

13

Unless dredged regularly, estate lakes diminish in size from the moment the valley is flooded because of the massive leaf fall from the great oaks, willows and beech which surround them. The build-up of fallen leaves can be clearly seen here at the dam end, where surplus water escapes during the winter when levels are considerably higher.

trout. This they try to solve by pandering to the trout's aggressive streak and using large gaudy, highly visible lures, rather than attempting the impossible task of imitating such a tiny natural food item as the daphnia.

I did once try to overcome this by taking with me to the lakeside a vacuum flask of hot water, a small fine mesh net and a packet of aspic. A net full of neat daphnia was then added to the hot water and aspic and stirred in the bottom of the bait tin and allowed to set. One hour later a ¾ in cube of daphnia, the nearest I could offer to a shoal of the real thing, was lowered on a size 8 hook to 5 lb test amongst a group of tench which were lying on the bottom, absolutely gorging themselves on daphnia. I would love to conclude by saying that this strategy was a great success. It was not. However, the idea is well worth keeping on the drawing board.

Estate lake tench are as a rule reasonably predictable and readily succumb to all simple methods and baits. Regardless of weather conditions and provided the weed is not beyond a normal summer's growth, the most effective method is to ledger with a swim feeder rig. This will hold and eventually draw tench into the desired area.

For close-in feeder fishing, that is for distances of up to 30 yards, it is sometimes worth pre-baiting the evening before, especially if planning a short session before work the next morning. For this, make up half a bucket full of special ground bait which should include a selection of the intended hook bait. Soak an old loaf, squeeze out the excess water, mash it to a pulp and stiffen the mixture with maize meal. To this add sweet corn, casters and hempseed. Making this up a few days beforehand allows the natural yeasts to start fermenting and gives the mixture a certain kick.

For distance fishing where the tench are way out – more than 50 yards – and where it is not possible to place ground bait accurately by throwing, it pays to rely on the precise and constant baiting to be obtained from using swim feeders.

To pick up line, often at great distances, I prefer to use an 11 or 12 ft 1¼ lb test curve, Avon-type rod in carbon fibre. These bend well with a hefty fish on close-in, yet remain fairly rigid and crisp in action for casting and striking. Generally it is preferable to have a two rod set-up in order to keep the feeders going in on a regular basis, even when bites are not forthcoming.

Tench react to the splash of the feeder hitting the surface and the free food its arrival heralds. To fish, noises can occasionally be an enticement rather than a warning, and once tench learn to associate feeders with a free meal they home in on them very quickly. For this method clear, open-end feeders are best, with a simple fixed paternoster rig. Coarse breadcrumbs form a very effective plug at each end and the contents explode attractively around the hook bait on impact with the bottom. A tip here is to dampen them only slightly or the feeder will clog.

Baits which work just as effectively as feeder fill as they do on a hook are maggots, sweetcorn and casters. Maggots, however, do have a tendency to wriggle into the thick silt on the bottom rather quickly. The solution is to scald a few in boiling water for a couple of seconds. Of course this means that they look rather stretched, but tench enjoy them just the same.

Should the tench start to become finicky after several sessions, try a change of bait in the feeder: stewed wheat, rice (dyed red or orange), hempseed, tares or mini boilies. Boiled and peeled saltwater shrimps are good; and it pays to experiment with hook baits as well. Tench love 'cocktail' baits like a bunch of maggots tipped with a couple of brandlings. Shrimp and caster or brandling and sweetcorn always prove popular, as does a lump of breadflake with a couple of maggots

15

wriggling through. Since the feeder is plugged with breadcrumbs, plain old breadflake is always a good standby and often sorts out the better quality fish, as indeed will a big lobworm.

To achieve extra buoyancy when fishing over a layer of bottom weed (and don't be afraid of weed), thread a small piece of breadcrust or a mini poly ball over the eye of the hook before putting the bait on. This is very effective. It is also a good idea to give a lobworm a little air from a hypodermic needle. Inject into the head so that it floats enticingly upwards, just above the bottom weed level and the tench will make straight for them. Remember, for lobworms and breadflake, increase hook size to a 6 or 8. For all other baits use a size 10 to 14. Only when the bites slow up, or the tench become suspicious should you switch to small hooks and a much lighter hook link.

At this time the standard ploy of using a hook length greater than the feeder link should be reversed. This is especially so if maggots or sweetcorn come back sucked to bits without so much as a twitch having been registered on the indicator. Condensing the terminal rig to a 5 inch hook link and 10 inch feeder link will immediately improve bite indication. However, don't just rely on the indicator moving. In calm conditions watch the line where it enters the water and hit instantly any tiny tremble or twitch, whether it lifts momentarily or drops back a little.

Twitching the bait along the bottom with one turn of the reel handle and resetting the indicator quickly will sometimes bring immediate

Tench must want anglers to catch them. During the early morning their distinctive feeding bubbles can clearly be seen in the surface film as they root down below through the rich organic bottom detritus of leaf mould and decaying plants, for blood worm and other aquatic goodies.

action. Tench hate to let their bait, especially worms, get away. By juggling around with baits and their presentation it is often possible to keep tench feeding throughout the entire day, especially in really warm, windy weather. A nice choppy surface is always an advantage; the line sinks quickly, surface draw is reduced, and threatening images or shadows which can be seen by fish through clear water are broken up. To sink line quickly in a flat calm, keep a small bottle of neat washing-up liquid to hand and apply it to the spool now and then. It makes all the difference.

For the continual casting and retrieving necessitated by feeder fishing

Dawn, the time when tench are most readily caught from estate lakes.

17

which can prove very hard on your tackle, go for a reel line of 6 lb test. Hook lengths can of course be varied according to hook size and how the tench react on the day. In heavy weed it is safe to stick with 6 lb test all the way through to the hook. Remember always to position the rod rests high above the surface when fishing on to a clear area beyond weed beds. This results in much better line pick up on the strike and consequently a better ratio of hooked fish to bites missed. Bite indication is regularly hampered where the line actually rests over weed, resulting in a reduced movement of the 'bobbin', so be prepared at all times to hit 'twitches'. This means one single 'bleep' on a buzzer if using an electric bite indicator of the 'roller type' such as the Optonic. Don't wait for anything more.

In very exceptional circumstances, where weed is particularly dense or coarse, don't be afraid to go up to an 8 lb test reel line, especially if the lake also holds a fair head of carp. The modern trend of using boiled baits for carp has, in mixed fisheries, resulted in the tench developing a taste for them too. This does not mean, however, as some anglers imagine, that tench will not then respond to feeder tactics; indeed, the reverse may be true. If everyone is using boilies and boltrigs on the lake,

LEDGERING OVER
WEED IN SHALLOW
ESTATE LAKES

RIGHT

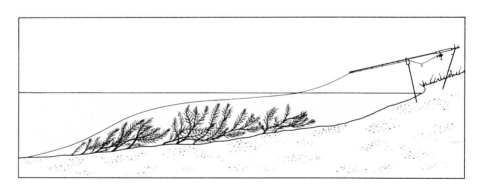

WRONG

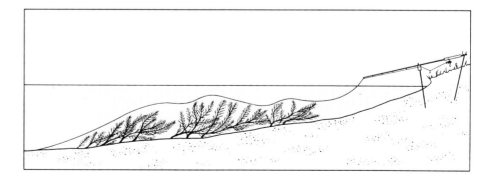

feeder fishing will prove more successful, because it is different.

When a particular area of the lake goes off because of over-fishing or because the tench have simply moved into deeper, shallower or warmer water, be prepared to move with them. Some estate lakes are so large you could try a different area on every trip and never have covered the whole extent during a summer. Shoals are very much larger with up to a hundred tench or more occupying a feeding ground. There is always plenty to go for.

In small estate waters of up to three acres, shoals are invariably limited, and you should be content with half a dozen tench for a good catch. There are exceptions, but as a rule the more tench there are, the smaller will be their average size. This is especially true in lakes holding fair numbers of bream and/or carp since these fish tend to dominate the food chain. It is perhaps worth mentioning that in estate lakes holding shoals of quality bream and no tench, these feeder tactics are equally effective for luring and holding the shoals to a given area. The same baits and ground baits will be effective although bream prefer breadflake or worm above all others. Night fishing in most estate lakes usually produces much better catches of bream, especially in those which are very clear. Night is also the best time for encountering those whopper rudd of 2–3 lbs which estate lakes have the habit of producing. Again, feeders work well for luring the shoals, but stick to a straight breadcrumb feed in the feeder and a large lump of breadflake on the hook. Using meaty baits such as maggots or worms after dark is just asking for eels to appear on the scene.

Night fishing does occasionally, and again particularly in gin-clear lakes, seem to be the best time for a real bag of tench, though if you feed consistently from a dawn start, daytime sport can usually be guaranteed. Provided they have the sanctuary of weed beds close by or coloured water, tench love to feed periodically all day, though their tell-tale feeding bubbles will ease up as sun comes upon the surface.

Float fishing

At the deepest, dam end of estate lakes, float fishing close-in is very often the most effective method, and in the right hands can easily outfish the feeder. For this the good old 'lift' rig is unequalled, and I would recommend swapping feeder rods for a lightweight 13 or 14 ft match rod and a 3 or 4 lb line. This deeper water also allows the tench to prove its mettle on lighter tackle, so don't be lazy and stick to ledgering. Enjoy the challenge of casting your float to individual patches of bubbles as they rise to the surface. Within seconds you will very probably be treated to an instant lift once the bait has settled.

19

opposite 'Now open wide sir, you won't feel a thing.' To avoid the large needle-sharp teeth which line the pike's lower jaw, an industrial glove on the left hand aids safe unhooking with long-nosed forceps.

This is the beauty of the method, especially when the rod is held throughout. You can hit bites you would never bother to strike or ever stand a chance of hitting when ledgering.

When tench are bubbling away naturally close to the dam wall, don't shovel in mountains of ground bait. The odd small ball won't go amiss, but endeavour to keep them feeding by weaning them away from bloodworms on to your items of loose feed. Sweetcorn is a good bait for this, because you do not have to suffer a shoal of immature roach or rudd appearing on the scene and taking the bait on the drop – a common occurrence if using casters or maggots in deep water.

The secret of fishing the lift method is encouraging the float to do exactly that, lift upwards when a tench sucks up the bait and dislodges the shot set just 3–4 in from the hook. The trouble is that the vast majority of anglers I see trying the lift have their waggler float fixed to the line between two locking shots, which completely defeats the object. There should be no shots whatsoever anywhere near the float, otherwise it cannot lift effectively. It should be attached to the line with a piece of silicon float rubber at the bottom end only. A simple length of plain peacock quill with just the tip dipped in red paint makes the best float for lift fishing. It has wonderful buoyancy and what could be more natural sitting in the surface film than a bird quill?

Cut a length of quill down to size with a pair of scissors so that whatever size shot you have close to the hook, just a quarter of an inch shows above the surface. Then set it slightly over depth so that you have to wind down to cock it once the shot and bait are resting on the bottom. From this point onward the slightest movement of the shot will register whether the float lifts or disappears. And if it lifts upward the float actually supports the weight of the shot until it lies flat, instead of the tench. It is very simple and effective. So remember, to enjoy text book tenching, no shot up the line.

A good indication as to the ultimate size each particular lake may produce in tench is to consider the size to which its male tench grow. Whenever males are regularly caught over the 4–4½ lb mark, for instance, a real monster female is on the cards. Lakes which turn up males in the 3½–4 lb class will usually produce a nice sprinkling of females over 5 lbs plus the odd 6 pounder. Estate lakes may not produce those monstrous double figure tench which are nowadays to be found in certain reservoirs and mature gravel pits, but for good numbers of handsome fish of very high average size, estate lakes take some beating. Gazing at the unbelievable colour of rhododendron bushes or watching the deer come to the water's edge at dusk and dawn makes tench fishing in estate lakes an experience second to none, often for the very modest price of a day ticket or season permit.

3
Gravel Pits
For Pike and Bream

Although gravel pits, particularly large ones, often appear uninteresting, uniform and seemingly featureless to anglers who can easily relate to the charms of a tiny pond or stream, these man-made fisheries do in fact hold the key to freshwater fishing of the future. As our river systems decline still further, we shall rely to a very large extent upon the wealth of old sand and gravel workings. Indeed, we are doing so already, for more and more clubs are today obtaining long leases to pits – stocking and landscaping for the future.

So instead of being intimidated by these huge sheets of windswept water, learn to understand them. Beneath the ruffled surface pits do not differ from other still waters. Certainly many pits are quite deep, down to 20–30 ft or even more. But they have individual features, too, close to which fish prefer to live and feed – like channels between islands, along deep gullies from which the richest stone deposits have been excavated, in sudden 'drop-offs' from shallow plateaux into deep water, or around deeper plateaux with shallows on three sides and, on the fourth, an equally deep connecting channel. Sunken and overhanging trees, thick reed lines, huge beds of surface plants, even old pieces of machinery sticking out from the surface – are more obvious potential fish-holding spots. All are worth exploring when seeking pike from gravel pits.

When investigating a new and previously unfished pit, if I cannot get out on the water in a dinghy and echo-sound the bottom, I spend time plummeting to obtain a mental picture of the topography for future visits. I may not even get around to fishing on that first day but it's always time well spent. Chuck it and chance it tactics are hopeless for

DEPTH FINDING
Fishing a large spoon and 'counting' it down, allowing 3 seonds per metre (1 second per foot), is an effective way of plummeting a gravel pit while fishing.

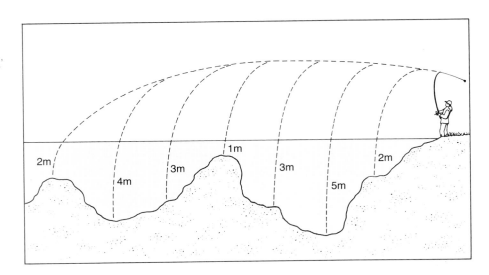

22

gravel pits. One of the most pleasant ways of exploring a new pit is to spend a day's lure fishing, using a large, heavy spoon. A spoon about 5 inches long, in either chrome or copper, is ideal because you fish as you plummet. It can be cast to distances of up to 60 yards and counted down to the bottom on each cast, allowing about one second per foot. If there is any soft bottom weed, the treble will certainly bring some back. So not only do you ascertain depths all over the pit but bottom structure as well. Casting repeatedly in a grid-searching fashion from various spots along the bank will provide invaluable information for future trips whether you decide upon lures or play the waiting game with a static dead bait. Sometimes it is worth drawing an outline of the pit and filling in the depths as you go.

Those shallow bars which rise sharply up from deep water on either side to within a foot of the surface are not areas where pike will find your dead bait in the depths of winter. So research well, for no two pits are ever dug exactly the same; each has its own character, its own balance and its own special mysteries.

During the summer all species tend to spread out, even over the shallowest bars and plateaux where they enjoy the food and protection provided by surface plants such as lilies or broad-leaved potamogeton. But when temperatures drop rapidly after a few hard frosts and the marginal growth disappears, most species want a good depth of water over their backs. Find perch in a deep gulley, for instance, and you will also come across small roach. Locate a strong head of quality roach and you can be certain that pike will not be far away, or vice versa; the best pike hot-spots invariably yield big pit roach as well. Sizeable bream are perhaps the exception, being as difficult to locate in low temperatures as they are easy to see in the warmth of summer, when they roll on the surface at dusk and dawn.

The most productive methods for catching quality sized pike from pits – fish, say, of over 10 lbs – is either dead baiting or lure fishing; or both. Searching an area with artificials on one rod, while presenting a static dead bait on the bottom on a second rod is both enjoyable and effective. Some days only the dead bait will score, sometimes the lures – but more often than not both will produce at various times of the day. With one static and one moving bait, a large one can be covered systematically; and whereas dead baits generally account for far larger pike, in particular the fat, lazy old females which relish the ease of sucking their meal up from the bottom, lures will often take greater numbers.

Even so, pike are unpredictable and their reactions to various baits seem to be affected by many factors. Wind direction, barometric pressure, water clarity and temperature, etc. all have a direct bearing on

Large chrome-plated or copper spoons are perhaps the most favoured of gravel pit lures, but plugs work well too. This pike took a liking to a banana-shaped shallow-diving wobbler.

For pike and perch like this striped 2½lb cracker, there is much fun to be had with the mobile approach using a short American-style rod and baby multiplying reel.

their movements and feeding habits. Yet they can still be induced to snatch at a live bait, wobbled dead bait or a lure if whisked near their nose, but you either need to be pretty sure of their whereabouts or spend numerous casts locating a taker. This is why artificial lure fishing, apart from being fun, is so effective; an enormous amount of water can be covered in a day.

The American influence

For several years the mobile approach, sophistication and expertise of American-style artificial lure fishing has influenced my attitude towards catching all predatory fish. Short, single-handed rods, multiplying reels, the vast choice of artificial lures from plastic worms to deep diving crank baits, and electronic fish-finding sonar equipment – all this may be a new ball game to the majority of British anglers but, believe me, the American influence is here to stay.

Compared to the guy who on every trip just sits there with two rods out, a dead bait on each, the lure enthusiast manages to learn so much more about his environment. He needs to, otherwise he'll lose an awful lot of expensive lures on snags he never knew existed or on the bottom which suddenly shelves up to a shallow gravel bar or thick weed bed where it wasn't supposed to.

In our Spinners, Spoons and Gadgets programme in Series Two of 'Go Fishing' I was able to show my 12-ft customised boat specifically designed for lure fishing. It incorporates a sonar fish finder, the versatile Humminbird 4-1D unit, which operates from a 12-volt battery by sending ultrasonic signals through the transducer, mounted in the rear of the boat below the waterline, at 5,000 cycles per second. The signals hit the bottom, plus any fish present within the radius of the beam, and bounce back through the transducer to the liquid crystal display screen, where they show up as dots. The fish appear in red as opposed to everything else in black. It really is quite wonderful and sometimes I just row about watching the read-out without even bothering to cast.

Making use of this modern piece of equipment has even been condemned as cheating, as if the fish simply crawled up the rod after being located. When you set off afloat in the early morning in the rain on a huge, previously unfished sheet of water, that is the last thing you worry about, believe me. The swivel chair, standard equipment on all American fishing boats, is simply an old office chair with the pedestal base removed. The stem, 1½ inches across, slots through a hole drilled into the centre seat and down into a reinforced gimble set into the bottom of the boat, allowing me to operate with or without the chair. I must admit, however, to using it on every trip. It is so comfortable, its height – compared to that of normal boat seats – does away with leg-ache, and I can angle the rod top down nicely on the retrieve, which is most important for lure fishing.

Also incorporated in the boat's design is a reinforced plate on either side of the transom on top of the gunnel to take a pair of downriggers. This marvellous American invention allows the bait to be presented in exactly the way its name implies – downrigged. The bait, a mounted fish or artificial lure, is rigged for trolling with a quick-release clip fixed to a heavy lead ball. The ball is lowered to any pre-selected depth via a strong cable wire and winch which has a depth counter calibrated in feet. The bait is then trolled behind the boat in the horizontal plane by oars or by outboard engine, enabling an enormous amount of water to be covered. When a predator grabs the bait, the lure pulls free of the downrigger clip and you have the delight of hooking and playing the fish on standard gear, instead of the previously used lead core lines and fixed heavy trolling weights.

Back now to lures and the types to use in various situations. As mentioned, big heavy spoons are great for fishing deep, distant areas. Where bottom weed rises to within just a few feet of the surface, simply opt for a much lighter version. Bar-type spoons such as the Toby and all its variations are excellent all-round lures because they come in a variety of different weights.

Deep diving/floating plugs, easily identified by their huge lips or vanes, are terrific for exploring deep gullies, interspersed with shallows, because when you stop winding they float up over the bars. For purely deep water work, however, totally sinking plugs are required. These may be counted down just like spoons and the retrieve started at the desired depth. Mid-water vibratory divers, of which the 'banana' type plug is just one, and those incredible, strange-looking spinner baits are both particularly good in coloured water because they can be retrieved very slowly. To the large single hook of my spinner baits a size 6 treble hook is wired in to alleviate takes which 'come short'. This does tend to spoil the spinner bait's 'weedfree' properties, but you can't have it both ways. Proper surface lures do not really dive at all. They gurgle, pop, plop, splash, twitch and sway, or whatever you make them do. That's the fun and it all depends on you.

Talking of rods, I prefer a crisp action 9 ft carbon for presenting most large artificials. Sloppy rods are useless. I point the tip at the lure throughout the retrieve, perhaps holding it just a little to one side when twitching and jerking. This results in real solid thumps and a far greater ratio of fish hooked than if the rod were held at right angles to the lure as it is when river ledgering. There is such stretch in monofilament that more pike come adrift within seconds of grabbing hold because the hooks never went home in the first place than for any other reason. (It goes without saying that hooks should be kept sharp by regular honing on a small stone.) Don't worry about the line snapping when a pike really hits the lure; just keep that rod up from round one and don't let it have an inch of slack line.

I rate a reel line of around 11 lb test adequate for working lures except for pulling surface poppers through tough lilies, then I step up to 14–15 lb test. Wire traces are 10 inches of 15 lb braided elasticium, with an American snap at the business end for quick lure changing.

The fixed spool is probably more versatile than the small multiplying reel, especially when it comes to putting out extremely light lures a long way, but multipliers always offer more fun. There is nothing more rewarding than flipping a tiny lead-headed spinning jig, diving plug or spoon between lily pads or beneath overhanging trees with a 5½ ft American bait-casting outfit. The terminology, however, is confusing because only artificial lures, not bait, are presented with these short, single-handed sticks and baby multipliers. Yet plastic worms rigged with a large single hook, the point just nicked into the soft plastic to make them 'weedless', can drive pike and perch absolutely wild.

Although their design was originally geared to the American family of sunfishes, which includes small- and large-mouth basses, British predators such as trout, chub and zander eagerly snap them up.

The thing to remember about working artificials is that they are exactly that. Without jerks, plops, twitches, slow winds, pulls, lifts, quick winds, gurgles, pauses, etc., they are simply pieces of metal, wood or plastic. The successful lure angler is ever aware of this fact and throughout the retrieve must imagine that a pike is following. A sudden, lively movement imparted to the lure is all that is needed for it to lunge and grab hold.

I try to play each fish to a standstill so that it can be lifted out by hand. Treble hooks caught in the mesh of a landing net cause havoc. Gaffs are barbaric and now, fortunately, outlawed. So there is no cleaner way of landing fish than by hand. But use a glove and keep your eyes on those trebles. Just slip your fingers (left hand if right-handed) into the pike's left gill slit and pinch hard down on the outside with your thumb. It can now be lifted out with its jaws already nicely open for unhooking. Hold a pike in the same way for unhooking regardless of how it was caught.

Dead baiting

As with lures, mounted dead baits can be worked very effectively in gravel pits and often score where lures fail because they are the real thing. My first choice, however, for big old pike is the static dead bait. A

Presenting a dead bait beneath a sliding float set well overdepth so that it lies perfectly static on the bottom, consistently produces larger than average size pike.

freshly killed fish lying naturally on the bottom offers the least suspicion of all. But the bait does need to be fresh and well presented. Those ledgered on too tight a line or beneath a float set exactly at swim depth, so that the bait lifts unnaturally every few seconds as the float bobs in the waves, do not catch many large pike. Pike learn through natural caution to associate certain things with danger, and dead fish which move when they shouldn't is one of them.

When boat fishing with the bait downwind, or fishing from the bank into deep water with the wind at my back, I use a sliding float (of the line through the middle type) set well over depth with the line well greased from float to rod. Twice or even three times swim depth ensures that the bait lies static and the float flat – not cocked. This is most important because when a pike sucks up the bait and moves off, the float simply follows behind, moving across the surface. There is not the slightest inkling of drag to make an edgy pike drop its prey. Alternatively, in gusty conditions for fishing across the wind in shallow lakes where underwater tow is a problem for fishing at long distance, a freelined bait is the answer.

Three swan shot are pinched on to the trace (as they are even when float fishing) next to the swivel to ensure the bait gets down quickly and to give the pike something to move against. It will then almost always move off against the direction of the rod, thus giving a positive run without fear of gorging the bait on the spot, resulting in a deeply hooked pike. Indication at the rod is optional – drop-off indicators, bobbins, monkey climbers, etc. – it matters little, so long as the pike can pull line freely from the spool without resistance.

A two-rod set-up is advisable for searching as much ground as possible. Mine are 12 ft long in carbon with a 2 lb test curve, and as with lure fishing I stick to an 11 lb test line. For picking up line on the strike, 12 ft is a good length, as I often put the bait out distances in excess of 70 yards. There are days when pike are really on the move and come to your dead bait no matter where it is cast, and other times when you must move the bait to them and literally hit them on the nose before any interest is shown.

Where bottom weed is troublesome, as it often is even in the depths of winter in clear watered pits, try injecting a little air into the back of the bait with a hypodermic syringe. Or push a 2-inch length of ⅜-inch diameter balsa dowel down the bait's throat. It will then lift up enticingly off the bottom, though it remains anchored by the three swan shot. Sometimes additional weight here is necessary.

The bait is in all cases mounted with the point of one treble in the tail root and the second treble along the flank; again anchored by just one point – simple yet effective.

Dan Leary from Lenwade in Norfolk cradles one of the largest pike ever to be caught from a gravel pit. This 39½lb monster, taken on a static dead bait, proves that intimate knowledge of the pike and its environment is essential.

I have little time for fancy rigs because I feel that if you have confidence in where you have placed the bait, and it is fresh, then pike will come. I particularly like half baits. It may seem unnatural for just the head end or the tail end to be lying there on the bottom, but pike don't see it in this way. To them a dead fish, or part of a dead fish, is a meal; and half baits, apart from allowing the inside juices to escape, offer excellent hooking prospects. There is no need to wait before striking, as you might with a large whole dead. (To allow instant striking, I always use small whole dead baits anyway.) Fish in the 5–7-inch range, small mackerel, herrings, sardines, smelt, scad, mullet and any other silver sea fish, and oddities such as red mullet and sand eels are also worth a try. With natural freshwater baits, eels, roach and small bream are my favourites.

For clear water conditions dyeing baits can be fun, the most effective colours being yellow, orange and red. Blot off the excess water with kitchen roll and use the same powder dyes, mixed with a little water, that are used in carp baits. Simply brush it on both sides and allow to dry before popping a day's supply of baits into the freezer. Don't forget to wrap them individually in cling film; it's worth the bother. On hard-fished waters any little ruse will produce more runs, and colouring dead baits is one trick up your sleeve.

Clear-water gravel pit bream are quite unlike the species in most other habitats. Immensely thick in cross section with huge blue-black fins, they fight like tigers. Look at the powerful lines of this 9½ pounder, caught on sweetcorn fished amongst the weed beds immediately below the rod tip.

Bream – the roving approach

Gravel pits really do suit bream, which in certain environments grow very large indeed. Bream in excess of 10 lbs nowadays come more frequently from pits than from any other type of fishery. It is dangerous to generalise, but as a rule heavily coloured gravel pits with minimal soft weed growth tend to breed mountains of bream of several year classes, ranging from skimmers to fish of modest proportions – up to 5–6 lbs. And the clear water of weedy, mature gravel workings allows the sunlight through to stimulate a prolific weed growth and subsequent rich pickings of zooplankton such as daphnia and midge larvae.

These are ideal environments for bream to reach specimen proportions, certainly into double figures, with a good sprinkling of fish in the 7–9 lb bracket. Shoals are rarely large but then a fishery can only support so many fish of a certain size, or feed so many mouths. Bream themselves tend to be self-cropping and in the clear water mop up most of their own spawn within a short time of it being laid, so that very few young bream ever come through each year to compete for the available food source. Inevitably, only one or perhaps two particular year classes and separate shoals enjoy a super-rich habitat, getting larger and larger. Eventually their deep flanks are too much even for the jaws of a large pike, so they have few natural enemies.

Pits containing shoals of these big old bream are not common because of increasing competition, in the form either of tench or carp, or both, which will dominate the food chain and thus retard the bream's weight potential. So it is worth searching around for a mature pit fishery where large bream are the dominant species and have things very much to themselves.

Follow up reports in the angling press of big bream catches in your area. Ask your local tackle dealer or fellow club members. Or do all the spadework yourself, during the latter part of the close season, by visiting any potentially good pit and searching with polaroid glasses and binoculars. Mature pits dug during the last war offer the best prospects.

This kind of bream is obviously going to be much harder to tempt than one competing for food in a shoal 200 or 300 strong. Clear water creates innumerable problems with bait presentation, especially in shallow pits which warm up quickly, becoming almost choked with weed halfway through the summer. Because of this and because it is virtually impossible to locate a small shoal of albeit big bream during the winter months, much of my big bream fishing is in the early part of the season when they are at least visible. Location, the most difficult aspect with most species, is often solved by the bream itself when they

A magnificent brace of gravel pit bream taken by the author on float tackle close in to the margins, together weighing almost 20lbs. A bunch of slowly sinking brandlings was their downfall. Note the spawning tubercles on the male's forehead. (Right)

opposite Proof of the value of stealth. A mirror and a leather, both over 20lb, caught in a short pre-work session on surface floaters amongst thick surface weed, mere feet from the bank.

roll on the surface at dusk and at dawn. Those lovely great bronze backs breaking through the surface film are a wonderful sight.

My methods are simple. I track the shoal's movements visually, waiting for an opportune moment, when it browses in one spot, to introduce a little loose feed and follow in with float tackle. Heavy balls of ground bait are the easiest way of scaring these clear-water fish.

The water they inhabit is so rich that they do not really need our offerings. But when presented in a natural manner and virtually on their noses, the hook bait will get sucked in. Worms fished 'on the drop' beneath a float are without question an ace bait, the gyrating movements inciting the bream into acceptance. The addition of a single grain of sweetcorn on the bend of the hook prevents the brandlings from wriggling off, and its colour alone, I am sure, helps to promote bites. Loose feeding with a little corn therefore completes the technique. Other baits, such as a bunch of maggots and especially breadflake, because it is so highly visible, also work well; on occasion you can actually see a bream suck it in. This is real roving fishing where mountains of tackle merely get in the way – often the shoal will only stay in one spot for a few minutes so there is not enough time even for pushing in rod rests.

When it suits them, bream can bite quite fast and so you need to strike quickly. Holding the rod and continually casting is the answer. When they feed among lilies or cabbages, alongside sunken willows, etc., bites can be most positive, the float simply sailing straight under. Generally I use a peacock waggler, set slightly shallower than swim depth, with most of the shot bulked around the float. A small shot around mid-depth is sometimes useful to pull the bait through lily pads.

When the shoal comes close to marginal weed beds I use a centre pin reel, for it needs only an underarm flick to reach them. Otherwise a small fixed spool reel with a delicate clutch suffices. Either way a 4 lb test line is ideal, with size 10–14 hooks tied direct.

The rod I use is a 14 ft three-piece carbon match with a progressive yet powerful action. Big clear-water bream show a surprising turn of speed and can really pull hard. So spliced tip match rods and light lines are out. A good way to induce bites is to pull the float back a few feet every minute or so, allowing the bait to rise up and free fall down again. Invariably the bites come on the drop, so concentrate hard and be ready, levering a hooked bream quickly away from dense lilies or thick weed. As a rule these hit and hold tactics are not required when bream fishing, so for most anglers this approach is unique. It can produce the very largest of still-water bream even at mid-day when they are not supposed to feed in earnest. Heavy ground baiting, fishing after dark and a long wait is not the only way of catching them. Believe me!

4
Lakes and Ponds
Stalking the Carp

There is nothing I love more during the summer months than stalking carp from intimate little waters – anywhere really, from village ponds to man-made lakes. This preference probably stems from the fact that my early carp fishing for both crucians and wild carp was in tiny ponds, some no larger than a tennis court, and park lakes from one to three acres in size. Learning to stalk carp in these diminutive environments, especially where heavily overgrown banks provided little room for casting, offered an enormous challenge, teaching me the true value of being stealthy and just how close into the margins it was possible to catch carp. Most species prefer to feed naturally along the marginal shelf because, being shallow, the water is always warmer, thus richer in aquatic plants and insect life. It is only we anglers with our clumsiness and noise who scare them out to distant areas. Then we have the bother of casting after them, which is daft. That's why I prefer the fun of close-range carping.

Wherever you fish, the first step is to identify all the various habitats carp are likely to frequent. In the case, for instance, of a large, unfamiliar lake, it is worth walking around, visually breaking the area up into small habitats and then concentrating on each as a separate entity, even though a tiny bay may be only one of several in a sprawling 60-acre lake.

Location

Even during the winter when the leaves have gone, marginal swims hold good prospects. Carp love the sanctuary of trees such as alders and willows whose lower branches lap the surface or, better still, actually submerge. Willows especially provide a wonderful home with a readily available larder of aquatic insects clinging to the fibrous matting of roots which sprout from the entanglement of sunken limbs. During the warmest months the green canopy overhead, in addition to diffusing the light, offers a rich natural food source in the way of caterpillars, moths and flies, etc. So a freelined bait, plopped in close beside the branches, often brings a natural immediate response.

Part-sunken hawthorns and blackthorns, though small, have dense foliage and thus immense attraction. Along with brambles, these bushes are sometimes the only available cover along the banks of ponds which are farmed right up to the edges. So they can be considered prime hot-spots, especially in bright sunny weather when carp love to browse underneath.

Apart from being the most beautiful of lakeside plants, the rhododendron provides yet another carp hide-out. The largest shrubs which hang well out over the margins, often right into the water, with a

Carp are far less suspicious of areas which have not been cleared so that anglers can cast easily. It is for this reason that simple float tackle presented close in amongst the trees is so effective.

depth of at least 2–3 ft beneath the leading foliage, are found only beside well established man-made lakes. Again, during the heat of a summer's day, if the carp are not visibly basking out in the middle or in the shallows, they will be hiding where the water is coolest, under the rhododendrons. The lower limbs of most other trees and shrubs do not usually get wet, but almost anything sizeable which falls into the water during a gale or through age is likely to attract the carp's attention.

Together with sunken trees, lily beds, whether marginal or some way out, are prime hot-spots. Even one tiny bed of lilies all on its own in a huge lake is enough to go for, because carp are always drawn to shade above and food below.

Tackle

For marginal work, most situations can be covered with only two outfits. One is an 11 or 12 ft carbon Avon rod with a 1¼ lb test curve coupled to 6 lb test. This is for smallish carp or for any encounter in coloured lakes which are completely free of snags and weeds.

The second is a 2 lb test curve 12 ft carbon with an all-through action coupled to 11 lb test. It is perfect for bouncing even large fish through snaggy swims and for an enjoyable fight with just about everything in more open water.

Hooks are particularly important for the hit and haul tactics very often dictated by margin fishing. When you cannot afford to let a fish run

35

more than a few yards, strong hooks are imperative. I use the Drennan super specialist and the Mustad 34021 O'Shaughnessy hooks for most situations, switching over to the Drennan lighter carbon specimens when there is more room for a drawn-out battle.

The only other item of tackle well worth mentioning is my 24-inch diameter, round, special deep mesh stalking/landing net. It has minnow mesh down the sides and a micro-mesh base to protect the fishes' fins and to stop split shot becoming caught. This net is great for manoeuvring through the tiniest gap where a large, traditional triangle net would easily become snagged, and can be held out with the pole fully extended over weed beds to net fish caught up in otherwise impossible situations. I once landed a 26¾ lb mirror carp in this 24-inch special which was stuck on top of a weed mat far beyond the reach of a heavier, traditional net.

Feeding carp

It is the available food source, and/or overhead cover from trees, bankside shrubbery, reeds or lilies, etc., which attracts carp even to comparatively small areas. And the best time for observing how they feed naturally is at dawn. Like tench, they spend a lot of time rooting in bottom silt for bloodworms, probing with their long barbels, which have taste pads at the ends, into the richest seams, often creating saucer-shaped depressions – such is the intensity of their feeding.

It is not always the weediest of waters which, as many anglers imagine, contains the most fish. Farm ponds, for instance, due to over enrichment from surface run-off, invariably contain such heavily coloured water that sufficient light cannot penetrate to stimulate the growth of soft weeds. Yet yard for yard they produce more fish than all other still waters. Much of the food source lives in the bottom detritus dominated by shrimps, *Asellus*, water boatmen and bloodworms. And on a typical summer's dawn, with a classical heavy mist hugging the surface, the pond's entire carp population goes on the rampage, sending up great lines and clusters of bubbles. Crucian carp, where present, can be distinguished by their clusters of tiny bubbles; they contrast with the lines of much larger bubbles which spew up to the surface as a mirror or wild carp furrows through the bottom sediment.

Watching the bubbles of feeding carp, however, can at times prove rather misleading because fish feed with different levels of enthusiasm according to the number of competitors they share with, coupled to the type of environment in which they live. For instance, in really weedy lakes choked with patches of soft weeds, where carp cannot move fast along the bottom, all you may see is the odd cluster of large bubbles, sometimes accompanied by a patch of discoloured water. If you watch carefully, another will suddenly appear shortly afterwards, not far from the first eruption. It is nevertheless the sign of a carp feeding with deliberate confidence.

Carp move and feed through thick lilies in the same methodical way, and even for quite close-range observation you require a pair of good binoculars to see those imperceptible movements of a flower stalk swaying gently or a pad bulging as a good fish browses beneath. Heavy glasses are difficult to hold for long periods; lightweight good quality glasses in either 8 x 30 or 10 x 40 magnification are absolutely perfect. Polaroid sunglasses and binoculars are as indispensable as the bait itself. After all, if you leave the bait at home you can always grub about for worms beneath tufts of earth or collect a supply of swan mussel from the margins; but forget the glasses and you really are in the soup.

Moving stealthily about through dense undergrowth with any more than a landing net and rod also creates problems. Odd bits of tackle and bait can easily be stored in jacket pockets; so even during the winter, provided it's not too cold, I wear only my waistcoat. Keeping quiet along overgrown banks needs practice. It is best to kneel rather than use a stool, and to employ rod rests only if absolutely imperative. As a lover of long trotting, which necessitates holding the rod perhaps for several hours at a time, I see no reason why carp fishing should not be the same. The only time I don't hold the rod throughout is when ledgering at long distance with a two-rod, wait-out set-up, which is not often.

After all, modern carp rods are so light that it seems crazy to put one

Tools of the trade are polaroid glasses and binoculars; perhaps more important than the bait itself.

in rests at the possible risk of a missed bite, always assuming that shoving the rod rests in haven't frightened off the fish in the first place. Besides, actually holding the rod stops laziness setting in – always a danger in carp fishing – and keeps the mind alert. It makes you impatient for a bite, which is a good thing because 'opportune' carp are the very essence of marginal fishing. One minute I may be laying on beside a patch of lilies with a couple of black-eyed beans or a peanut presented over a bed of hempseed, waiting for the float to lift, or watching a small dog biscuit floater cast into the middle of the lilies with the aid of a small controller float, and the next minute the picture changes completely. The glimpse of a tail pattern, bubbles or the sight of a good fish in a clearing a few yards away requires an immediate change of tactics. It takes but a second or two to remove float and shots. Then, with a gentle plop, in will go a freelined bait – a cockle, a lobworm or a lump of protein paste; and as it sinks slowly I study the line where it enters the surface for that sudden yet confident tightening.

Once the sole method of presentation, long before set method ledgering with hair and bolt rigs took over, 'freelining' is now sadly neglected by modern carp anglers. Yet those of us who keep faith know that it is both simple and effective. Even old-hat baits like breadflake, lobworms, luncheon meat, trout pellet paste, etc., scorned by today's trendy enthusiasts, will still produce carp when freelined.

On the drop, fishing is effective everywhere from deep, completely clear-water areas where groups of carp may be seen basking or cruising at mid-water, to overgrown, jungle-type swims where you can even stalk individual specimens – simply because the bait appears 'untethered'. Once again, the modern set-piece trend of anchoring the bait down on heavy leads, with lines wound up as tightly as a bowstring, is very often self-destructive – particularly at close range. Carp are inhibited by tight hawser-like lines because in their world nothing beneath the surface is ever rigid. All subsurface plants bend to their bodies as they pass between, which is why carp are quick to panic off, giving those sudden eruptions in shallow water that we call 'liners'.

On suitable occasions, nevertheless, I do use shock or bolt rig methods. I even gear the bolt routine to lift-float fishing, simply by having four or five swan shots fixed together on the line 4 inches from the hook. This stops nuisance species like tench and bream moving the bait about and giving false bites, as they can do with just a single shot. It's rather 'hairy' fishing, however, especially close to thick lilies or beside a jungle swim of branches or tall reeds. There is usually no warning. One second the float is there, the next you're playing a carp. So you need to have your eyes on the float throughout, and quickly get the rod up into a full bend before the carp bolts into snags.

As described in Chapter 1, the lift rig can also be devastatingly effective for carp. In those tight areas alongside or between sunken branches and gaps between pads, where a ledgered bait offers problems with casting and subsequent presentation, not to mention bite indication, the good old lift does it all and so ridiculously simply.

Attractor baits

To encourage carp movement through small areas on the edge of lily beds, beneath submerged trees or even in marginal swims in ponds and lakes which have few natural features, but where the water is well coloured, I love to pre-bait with stewed hempseed. Carp never seem to tire of this attractor, and quickly get their heads down to root about.

In heavily coloured waters, farm ponds, old marle pits, etc., which muddy up even more as a result of bottom disturbance, line bites on float tackle can pose a problem. So it's wise to strike only at definite lifts or steady dips of the float. Any sudden movements should be ignored when the area is packed with fish or a foul hooked carp might result.

Other excellent seed-type attractors are tares, wheat and maple peas. Each is simply prepared by covering with 2 inches of boiling hot water in an airtight plastic bucket and left overnight to stew. The excess water

left Preparing most particle baits like peas, beans, seeds, peanuts and grains is so easy. There is no need to stink out the kitchen or ruin a saucepan.

right Place into a bucket with a lid and cover with boiling water by two or three inches (to allow for expansion) adding colouring and flavour as desired. Press the lid firmly on, shake and leave overnight. Strain off the excess liquid and pop into polythene bags for immediate or future use. It makes sense to prepare large batches and store in the freezer.

is strained off in the morning and any surplus bait may be packed into poly bags and popped in the freezer for later use. Leaving each in its own juices in the bucket for a few days will certainly do no harm, for carp definitely seem to be turned on by the smell of naturally fermenting yeasts.

Other good float fishing particle hook baits such as peanuts, chick peas, black-eyed beans and the like are prepared in exactly the same way; but tiger nuts, a lovely bait to use, need to soak overnight in cold water and then be pressure cooked for 20 minutes. Large beans such as red kidneys, butter beans and borlotti are best used straight from the tin once the juices are strained off. There is no end to the variety of baits you can float fish for carp. Macaroni segments, peeled shrimps and prawns, even boilies. Where bottom weed poses problems to sinking hook baits, try a mini black or yellow boilie fished over a carpet of hempseed or a floating pop-up boilie. Simply increase the distance between boilie and bottom shot to accommodate weed depth, not forgetting to use extra shots to counteract the boilies' buoyancy.

Floating baits

Floater fishing, presenting small buoyant baits such as cat and dog biscuits, trout pellets, floating boilies, etc., is without question one of the most exciting yet frustrating methods of carp fishing. Unlike all other rigs, you can actually see the carp's reaction and watch in fascination as fish after fish repeatedly refuse yours while they continue confidently to suck all the others down.

Surface presentation is always difficult because whereas we always look down into darkness and the bottom of the lake, the carp is looking upward into brightness, with the terminal rig exceptionally well illuminated. Everything appears in silhouette form when the carp is directly below the bait, but from sideways-on the line and hook are plainly obvious. Just the weight of a strong forged hook is enough to sink floating baits down to an unnatural angle. Use as light a hook length as you dare, plus the lightest hook and the smallest of floaters. Try casters, for instance. Dark casters are more buoyant than light red or orange ones and really work well in bunches of three or four.

When frustration sets in, as it inevitably will, there are still a few ruses worth trying. When fishing right in among dense lilies, for example, wind the hook bait up on to the very edge of a pad so that the line rests across the pads and doesn't touch the surface; or dangle your bait straight down from the rod tip with not an inch of line touching the surface. This old-time method works wonders. But you need to be a stealthy stalker and hold a loop of line in the left hand which is taken up

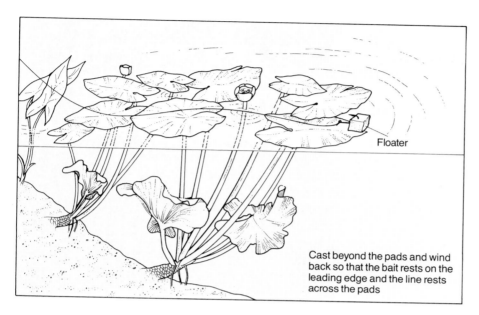

Floater

Cast beyond the pads and wind back so that the bait rests on the leading edge and the line rests across the pads

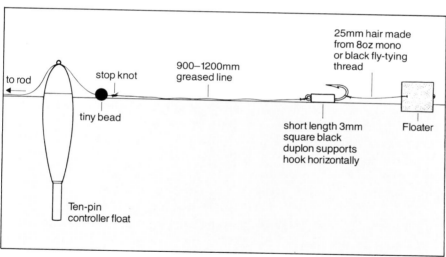

to rod

stop knot

tiny bead

900–1200mm greased line

25mm hair made from 8oz mono or black fly-tying thread

short length 3mm square black duplon supports hook horizontally

Floater

Ten-pin controller float

by the carp as it sucks the bait and gets its head down. Keep well back from the edge, with only a foot of the rod tip beyond the marginal growth or dangle it straight down into the tiniest gap between lilies. Either way it is great hit and hold fishing – probably carping at its best.

To place small, light floaters with accuracy into awkward spots I use a small controller float, the 'tenpin'. I actually designed this float for casting small dog biscuits from a gap between tall trees, using just an underarm flick, to a run alongside sunken branches 40 yards across the

41

opposite side of a small lake. But it works just as well at close range. The tenpin is stopped 3–4 feet above the hook by a small bead and sliding stop-knot, a ledger stop or a small junction swivel which permits use of lighter hook lengths. The line is then free to pass through the ring in the top of the float when a carp makes off with the floater. Fixing a stop on the other side to make the float 'fixed', rather like a surface bolt rig, helps to hook finicky carp. They tear off in panic and hook themselves.

Generally, however, I go for a more subtle approach so as to see the carp close its great lips around the floater and sink down beneath the surface before I bang the hook home. This is where a mini hair rig and floating hook set-up can help. Simply thread a short length of ⅛-inch square black duplon (rod handle foam) on to the shank of the hook, just enough to make it float instead of dangling beneath the surface. Then rig up a 1 inch hair from 8 oz mono or black fly, tying silk on to the bend of the hook, and attach the floater.

Fish which are repeatedly scared by floating baits, regardless of the subtle and ingenious rigs that anglers devise, are, ironically, absolute suckers for a slowly sinking one. This is because carp never get hooked when sucking waterlogged baits in 'on the drop', so their confidence grows. Even a small piece of freelined breadflake scores among a patch of totally ignored crusts. Try it and see. If it is dropping naturally, carp will grab it or wait until it's absolutely stationary on the bottom, then suck it up. Simply increase distance between controller and hook to slightly more than swim depth, and you will be in with a chance from the moment the bait lands on the surface, all the way down to the bottom. To make buoyant baits sink slowly, add a tiny shot a couple of inches from the hook.

Fun with crucians

To tempt the always obliging crucian carp, I step down to tackle which really allows this dogged battler to show its mettle: 13 foot carbon float/match rod, centre pin reel holding 2½ lb test and a simple lift float rig. A thin piece of peacock quill about 3 inches long which takes just one AA shot is absolutely perfect for close-in work and size 10–14 hooks directly tied, depending on bait, complete the rig. As crucians bite delicately, it is imperative to have the shot no further than 2 inches from the hook – and when they are really pernickety, just an inch away.

In 'crucian only' lakes I step down to a lighter rig with a no. 1 or BB shot and a slender float to match. Invariably, however, other species which breed prolifically in the kind of small ponds and lakes where crucians fare well, such as roach or rudd, restrict the use of ultra-light

Crucian carp Swedish-style. A bag of plump two pounders taken during a 'Go Fishing' programme from a lake in the suburbs of Karlstad. Breadflake and corn fished 'lift' style did the business.

tackle. Indeed, use a single maggot or caster on most waters and the crucians will never get a look in. It is best, therefore, to offer a reasonably neat hook bait such as a couple of grains of sweetcorn on a size 12 or a piece of breadflake just covering a size 10. See what happens – you can always scale down, as indeed you will be obliged to as the crafty crucians become increasingly suspicious.

Hitting any slight movement of the float is the answer with this fish, whether it lifts imperceptibly or gently dips. Sometimes the quill even comes flying up and lies flat in a glorious classical lift bite. But crucians

43

opposite Nearly five hundred miles long, running through Norway and then Varmland in south-western Sweden, the wonderful Klaralven River offers superlative trotting sport for roach, ide, dace, trout and whitefish. Here in the breathtaking upper reaches at Branas, a raft may be hired whilst your car is driven downriver some 80 miles to where the rafts finish their week-long drift.

seem to become very cunning indeed after a while, so I wind the float down until it's a mere 'blimp' on the surface, and hit anything. Moving the bait slowly along the bottom for a few inches sometimes stimulates an immediate grab. And using a 'cocktail' such as a brandling topped with a grain of corn will often promote more aggressive bites. You need to keep trying something different all the time.

Prolific crucian fisheries are invariably lily-covered, reed-lined and not too deep; between 3 and 6 feet seems the ideal depth range for this golden rounded carp. I chose two such classical lakes for 'Go Fishing' Series Two and Three. One was a rambling willow-clad club water near Norwich, the other – about 12 acres, large as crucian fisheries go – lay right among the suburbs of Karlstad in the county of Varmland in south-west Sweden. An odd location, perhaps, for catching crucians, but what wonderfully shaped fish they were – and all between 2 and 3 lbs. I have never before or since caught crucian carp so thick across and deep in the body. In British waters they tend to overpopulate for their own good, ending up rather slim in the body; but these were exactly like an artist's painting of ideal crucians.

In small overcrowded ponds or lakes that lack predators, stunting is a regular phenomenon, with the entire stock ending up just 7 or 8 inches long or even smaller, and never growing any larger.

In our Swedish lake, resplendent around the reed-lined margins with the most enormous beds of red and common yellow lilies, the crucians were kept in check by a healthy pike stock, which obviously accounted for the unusually high average size.

Using both flake and corn beneath a simple lift rig alongside the lilies, I took a catch of around twenty lovely fish in barely a couple of hours' filming. It was marvellous sport and might have been very much better had fate not taken a peculiar hand. The lake, despite its urban location, is rarely fished, so my guides in Sweden, Lars and Per, had been baiting an attractive tree-lined swim with corn for a few days before my arrival. However, by coincidence on the day prior to shooting, a group of Londoners on holiday and fishing the Klaralven River in Karlstad had seen the lake and decided to walk around. Furthermore, at that same moment, several large crucians decided to roll in the very swim baited for me. At the end of the day, just as Lars arrived to introduce the last batch of ground bait ready for the morning shoot, the six Londoners were pulling out their nets for a photo session.

That evening Lars had an awkward time trying to explain how two hundredweight of big crucians caught the day before might just alter our plans. Fortunately it made little difference and I think I could have gone on catching for the rest of the day. In fact, the Londoners, all very nice guys, turned up during the shoot and we shared a good laugh about it.

5
Big Rivers
Trotting for Roach

Extracting fish from a wide, deep and powerful river is the ultimate challenge for the freshwater float angler. In narrow rivers the flow pattern is usually easy to read and the fish-holding spots plainly obvious, but not so in a big, fast-flowing river. There are entire areas completely unsuitable for, and thus devoid of, shoal fish such as roach. So you must study the surface flow patterns. Be the roach small or large, you need to read each likely-looking stretch and search it thoroughly, first with your eyes and then your float – seldom are fish spread about like raisins in a well-baked cake. They relate to pressure of the current, whether steady or intermittent. Roach in particular prefer steady water, so ignore areas where tiny vortexes of water spiral up to the surface.

These swims may be inhabited by roach during the summer months when dissolved oxygen levels elsewhere in the river are low, but they will not thank you for such a winter home. Roach hate chasing food particles which get shot all over the place by spiralling currents. They like to intercept food casually as it drifts by close to the bottom and, of course, once it has sunk and lies static. You might say, with only a touch of fancy, that one good reason why the older, more lethargic specimen roach go for a large lump of ledgered breadflake in preference to all else is that they appreciate a square meal on the plate.

Flow patterns are not always easy to define with the naked eye, viewed sideways-on from the bank. Stand in the middle of a river bridge, look immediately downstream and you will see what I mean. In the main flow through the centre, always the fastest water, the current will follow a particular line for perhaps 30 seconds or so and then suddenly change a few degrees to the right or the left. It might be deflected by various features such as the bridge supports, an island, or a great pile of rubble (previous bridge supports) lying on the bottom and angling the water sharply upwards. This causes large, spiralling vortexes to churn the surface and is obviously a spot for roach to avoid, though salmon, trout and barbel love such habitats.

The flow slows dramatically as it nears each bank and is directly affected by bankside features; a reed-line reaching far out into the river, a large sunken tree, trees with branches that more than lap the surface, natural promontories, walls, moored boats, side streams, bays, entrance dykes, confluences and the like. There are numerous features that not only afford comfortable fishing from which to trot a float downstream but also create desirable accommodation for roach because of the steady flow. Wide bends in the river provide steady water on the inside, because the main flow is directed towards the outside of the bend. Usually the best spot to trot in these swims is that piece of 'filter' water on the edge of the slack just before the main current.

When you piece it all together there is much more to apparently

uniform big rivers than at first meets the eye. They are really not as hostile as first impressions indicate, so long as you learn to read the flow patterns.

One very friendly, convenient act that roach perform, especially at dawn and at dusk, is to cavort on the surface. On the wide, fast tidal stretches of my local Norfolk rivers Wensum, Yare and Bure, rolling roach are as much a part of dawn as the heron which departs as you arrive. On typically misty mornings in the summer and autumn and even on misty, frosty mornings throughout the winter, one of the best methods for locating the roach shoals of big rivers is to be there on the water in a dinghy as dawn breaks. It is a lovely method of fishing, being able to anchor directly upstream of the shoal and to trot a bait down to them. And for centre pin enthusiasts like myself, one of the most satisfying feelings in coarse fishing is to use the current, holding a stick float back just hard enough and to feel the line spin off the pin. You can overshot the float as much as you like so that the tip is a mere dot on the surface even when held back. The bait (casters or maggot) only just precedes the float, so bites are indicated immediately and when you strike, the fish is directly beneath the float.

Perhaps the most majestic of British trotting rivers is Scotland's mighty River Tay. This stretch is at Dunkeld where grayling and the occasional specimen roach are taken on long-trotted maggots.

Where river traffic is sparse, two anglers may sit anchored across the flow, both working the float along the same line. But amid holiday craft which are now dense all over Broadland's tidal rivers until at least the end of October, anchoring bows into the flow and sitting on the centre seat looking over the transom is recommended only for the lone angler.

We featured trotting for tidal river roach and all the associated river traffic problems in Series One of 'Go Fishing' when I visited the River Bure at St Benet's Abbey. I arrived very early in the morning for this shoot because it was imperative, from the filming aspect, to secure one particular anchorage. Unfortunately, a heavy mist blanketed the river from bank to bank so that by the time the film crew had motored downstream from Ludham Bridge they couldn't find me. I find that being afloat in thick mist is an exciting part of autumn fishing, although you do need to know the river well or you can end up in the wrong spot altogether. So I got a perverse pleasure from the plaintive cries of 'John, John' that came echoing through the mist as the 25-ft camera launch drifted eerily by.

The heavy mist at least kept most of the hire craft tied up for an extra hour or so, but it was short-lived. Anchored close by the fifteenth-century ruins of St Benet's Abbey, my little dinghy was soon bobbing up and down as one by one the cruisers ploughed up and down. Waiting until September to shoot, in the hope that boat congestion would be reduced, had been a complete waste of time. The day turned out like a Bank Holiday Monday, even in the middle of the week, but then that's Broadland. If you can't hack the other boats it's pointless getting another one out to go fishing. Besides, the roach and the bream don't jump out on the bank; they are still in the river even if the huge furrows, churned up by cruisers banging along at more like 10 knots instead of the permitted 5 mph, make it all the more difficult to catch them. Trying to film from a rocking boat was an additional problem, despite the fact that I had deliberately anchored only 15 yards away from a line of navigational posts to which the camera launch was firmly tied.

Inevitably, during much of the filming the crew had to abandon the launch and shoot from the bank; and even then half the footage could not be used because of the endless succession of holiday makers gawking at the camera or making obscene gestures. The lunatics cut us up just for the hell of it, and generally gave us a most difficult time. A typical day afloat on the Broads – no more, no less.

I am certain, nevertheless, that all this disruption benefited inasmuch as it identified a problem that you must come to terms with when fishing the tidal waterways. Another problem for dinghy fishermen is anchoring the boat exactly where you want to be. Remember to let out several extra feet on the upstream (bows) mudweight, although the aft

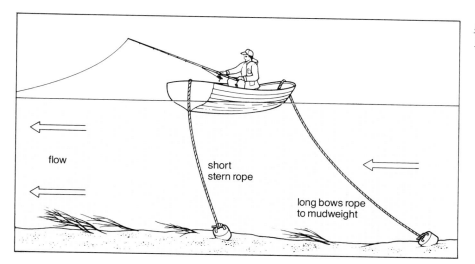

flow

short
stern rope

long bows rope
to mudweight

end one can be tied fairly tight. Remember also to loosen the latter one as the tide rises. The overall secret is using heavy mudweights in the first place, 30–35 lbs, spliced to a soft nylon rope of ½-inch diameter.

Of all the big rivers I have trotted, I would once have rated Scotland's Tay as the mightiest. That is until I visited Sweden and fished the Klaralven River. This monster watercourse spends the first half of its 500 miles flowing through Norway. It then enters western Sweden, running through the county of Varmland, where it travels in a southerly direction, eventually emptying its water into Lake Vanern, the third largest lake in Europe, and a veritable sea when the weather is rough. In the lower reaches, particularly around the delta upon which the city of Karlstad is built, the river contains not only bream, dace, perch and the fabulous golden ide, but also some massive concentrations of roach. Whilst individual specimens are rare, each shoal is so large that for hour upon hour it is almost a bite a trot. That's once you have located them – or rather the water which suits them – for this river fairly belts along and can span up to 300 yards across. Most of the channels within the delta, however, average around 100 yards wide.

Even in the high upper reaches, known better for its stocks of grayling, white fish and trout, the Klaralven can measure 200 yards across and average over 12 feet deep in many stretches. Add to this cut logs of pine and fir which continually drift downstream on their way to various paper mills en route, and it is indeed a real challenge to the long-trotting enthusiast. During the shooting of our Series Three programmes in Sweden I chose to fish in these beautiful but colder upper reaches, with their breathtaking scenery, at a spot called Branas,

49

where I actually fished from a raft. Complete with on-board tent, cooking utensils and anchor, this may be hired for a week or so while your car is driven back downstream some 80 miles to where the raft is eventually carried by the strong flow. It's a kind of trot as you go; and when the grayling are on, the fly fishing is superb too.

During our shoot, however, the river carried two extra feet of water due to an exceptionally early spring and prematurely melting snows where the river rises in Norway, so I had to settle for a whitefish called 'sik', a grayling look-alike, without the sail-like fin, which bites strongly to bunches of maggots or small red worm. In the Scottish lochs such as Loch Lomond they are known as powan, so I was surprised to find them common in the fast-flowing Klaralven River, having always associated them with huge deep-water lochs. I hooked one long two-pounder further downstream than I have ever previously hooked a fish trotting – some 60 yards if it was an inch. This was centre pin fishing at its very best with more than enough pull to revolve the pin smoothly and send a five swan shot loafer float steadily downstream for as far as the eye could see the tip.

My favourite centre pin, incidentally, is an old match aerial, but I also use a modern ball-bearing Adocks Stanton, which is equally free-running. On each is a specially made line guard from 18-gauge sprung stainless steel wire. It has cross bars, silver soldered across the drum to alleviate line that finds its way around the back of the reel, enabling me to feed line off in slow currents without consciously and repeatedly having to look at the reel. In strong currents the line is always under some tension and so the problem does not arise, but I urge any centre pin angler who does suffer line 'flap back' to construct a simple line guard.

Reel line for most of my trotting is 2.6 lb test, though I do have a couple of spare spools holding 3.2 lbs and 4.4 lbs should I be after, say, roach or grayling, and when a large chub, barbel or even a salmon is a possibility. For clear-water roach I step down to a 1.7 hook length and very occasionally even down to a pound bottom in slow, clear, extremely cold water when bites even fail to submerge an already well-shotted stick float.

It's always a case of horses for courses with roach and the continuous challenge of altering end tackle, hook size and shotting pattern until bites are induced. Tackle set-up is even more critical during the colder months when roach are much less susceptible to taking a moving bait. Only baits trotted slowly will be taken.

I also love to fish the waggler in big rivers, though generally in the deeper, slower stretches where the bait can be presented well over depth and dragged gently along the bottom. In my experience big roach

above In the relatively unfished waters of the Klaralven River system. John met his first sik — a whitefish called 'powan' in Britain. The sik accepted four maggots on a size 10 hook, trotted a long way downstream beneath a four swan shot loafer float.

left Most spectacular amongst Swedish freshwater species is the golden ide, a brilliantly coloured cyprinid which grows to weights in excess of 8lbs, and fights incredibly hard.

Trotting for roach from an anchored boat allows superb control of a stick float.

are more liable to be caught when waggler fishing because of the way the bait behaves. It trundles much closer to the bottom, compared to the stick which causes the bait to rise up each time the float is checked.

Only in exceptionally deep, fast water do I use groundbait feed, and then simply as a vehicle to ensure that the loose feed, either maggots or casters, get down quickly and do not feed up roach five swims further downstream. In deep water close in, I rely on the effectiveness of a bait dropper; and for all other feeding except close range, the catapult reigns supreme. Indeed, during really windy weather I dread to think where we would be without them. The only drawback with catapults is that loose feeding becomes too easy. The risks are that you may overshoot the line of trot, taking the fish out of the swim, and that you may overfeed. So, when first feeding the swim, it is worth concentrating on accuracy, to ensure that the bait lands far enough upstream to end up where you eventually want it to settle, and avoid putting any more in the pouch than you really need. The old adage of 'little and often' is the best tip any roach angler can pass on.

Many anglers trotting for roach don't like putting plenty of shot on the line and consequently choose a float which is too light for the flow. A lot

Anchoring a boat for fishing can pose problems. For filming it proved a nightmare. Fortunately John chose to fish close to a navigational post, allowing the crew to tie up immediately downstream and capture the action.

In rivers where roach and bream predominate there is often much confusion between true roach and roach/bream hybrids. This picture clearly shows all three. A bream, a hybrid, and a large roach.

opposite Whatever the weather, quiver tipping for chub during the winter months produces the goods. Be prepared for the tiniest registrations on the tip when temperatures are sub zero.

of shot might seem insensitive, but provided the float – any float – is correctly shotted with the bare minimum of the tip visible, roach bites will show. It's always better to use a float carrying more shot than the swim would appear to need, than one carrying too little. Steady, natural bait presentation is what trotting in a powerful flow is all about, and this cannot be achieved by a light, delicately shotted float which the flow 'zooms' along.

In deep, fast water where the bait needs to get down quickly to where the roach are holding just above bottom, I first bulk most of the shot within 4–5 feet of the hook and then attend to balancing with small shots in between.

In deep, slow swims more traditional ways of shotting may be used, such as spreading the shotting load evenly between float and hook with the stick, and bulk shotting around the stem of the waggler with just one or two smaller shots down the line.

A good guide for float selection is to look at the current speed, decide the amount of shot the swim will need to present the bait slowly, and then use a float which carries slightly more.

BIG RIVER TROTTING

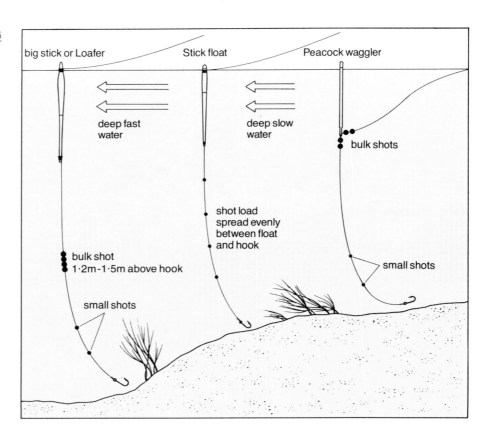

6
Small Rivers
Chub and Barbel

A fast, clear-flowing gravel and sandy-bottomed river with a prolific plant growth and an abundant source of aquatic food from shrimps to crayfish is every river angler's dream. Those overgrown along the banks with willows and alders, where beds of tall reeds or rushes shade and soften the marginal shallows, offering cover and beauty to fish and angler alike, are particularly cherished. And well might they be – it is the sad plight of many rivers today that water authorities should, in their infinite wisdom, see fit to remove character from the bankside under the dubious heading of river management.

They cut down overhanging willows whose lapping branches once offered protection to year-old fry during winter floods. They clear out dykes to expedite surface run-off and angle the banks back, removing sedges and rushes where shoals of small fish once found sanctuary. Farmers who clear and plant to within mere feet of the river, thus destroying bankside habitat, are equally to blame in the ruination of a river's natural character. And this all too often happens nowadays. Our rivers are suffering enough as it is through borehole water abstraction, treated sewage effluent, plus extra nitrates and phosphates. This is why the very best potential for chub and barbel remains in rivers largely left alone.

I therefore decided upon three such small rivers to illustrate the techniques of quiver tipping and long trotting in our 'Go Fishing' series: the wonderful Hampshire Avon on the famous Royalty Fishery in Christchurch; my local River Wensum near Norwich; and Worcestershire's lovely River Teme which meanders through picturesque hop-growing countryside famous for its rich red soil, eventually to feed the mighty Severn.

I have always associated small, clear-flowing rivers with picture books because each has a story to tell. For instance, to creep up on a shoal of barbel in a fast run close into the bank and to observe how they behave helps answer so many questions. You learn that sudden heavy 'plinks' on the rod tip are not bites after all, merely the barbel's large pectoral or pelvic fins momentarily catching the line as the fish moves across the bottom to take up a new position. You realise why a sandpapery sensation travels up the line to your fingers when touch ledgering immediately before the rod arches over. It is because the barbel moves its head from side to side, centralising the bait beneath its mouth, and the long barbels (tactile whiskers) do a 'plink-plonk' on the line.

There is a world of knowledge open to the stealthy angler who takes the trouble to look closely for clear-water barbel and chub. No doubt along the way the odd good shoals of roach, dace or bream will be located, and every so often the whereabouts of a particularly big pike

above Barbel love snaggy habitats, which is exactly what this huge fallen beech tree provided across an acute bend of the Upper Wensum, before the River Authority removed it.

left John took advantage of this feature and after free baiting with hempseed for several evenings prior to fishing, caught this monster barbel only an ounce short of 12lb. Bait was breadflake on a size 10 hook direct to 4lbs line, quiver-tipped just above the submerged branches as dusk fell.

can be noted, and perhaps tried for later on when the weeds have died down. That's the beauty of keeping in touch with a river. It is a living thing, varying on a day-to-day basis, and you need to read its many moods and observe its metamorphosis from summer to autumn, from autumn to winter and from normal conditions to high spate.

During the summer months I use the clear visibility to locate chub and barbel by sight. There is no more accurate method. Such findings lay the foundations for fishing later on during the colder months when the water is coloured and the weeds have gone. Even small rivers can appear daunting when full and flowing swiftly. Summer hours spent climbing trees and crawling about to look intently through polaroid glasses instead of actually fishing finally prove worthwhile when it is possible to pin-point the exact whereabouts of each species – chub-only swims, barbel-only swims, swims which hold the better specimens – and swims where both species share a choice run.

While it is true to say that in many rivers barbel and chub are regularly caught from the same swims, where they do have the option, barbel usually prefer a strong flow. They take up residence in the fastest currents, whether close into the bank between long flowing beds of streamer weed, in the middle of the river between beds of bulrushes, beneath an overhang of alders or willows, or in open, deeper water.

Chub are nowhere near so fussy and can even be encouraged upstream well away from their hideouts by careful free baiting, even during the winter months when there is little cover. Most of my favourite upper Wensum chub haunts have few trees along the banks, and the clumsy summer angler could easily walk along believing, as some undoubtedly do, that there isn't a single chub in the river. But they are there alright, resting in the subdued light beneath the marginal matting of sweet reed grass which grows out upon its own rootstock. These floating hideouts often reach several feet into the river and can harbour enormous chub shoals.

Obviously, wherever there is a deep gulley beneath overhanging trees on the outside of a bend, chub are bound to be in residence, as they are beneath summer rafts, formed by cut weeds caught against trailing branches. It's not just the supply of falling insects; chub simply love a roof over their heads.

Quiver tipping tackle

Taking into account all the varying types of swims frequented by barbel and chub, summer and winter, I consider the most productive method to be quiver tip ledgering. An 11 or 12 ft carbon Avon with a built-in quiver tip is the best tool for the job, matched with a small fixed spool

Painting the last 20 inches of the quiver tip matt white shows up the tiniest of bites.

reel holding 5–6 lb test. The top 20 inches of the rod, in fact the entire quiver tip, is painted matt white for detecting those shy bites in low light conditions or when an unpainted tip would otherwise get lost against certain backgrounds. It also picks up the light nicely from a narrow torch beam so that you can watch for bites at night, hour after hour, without eye strain. Always position the torch from the downstream side of the rod so that the beam shines upstream and away from the swim.

Terminal rigs are kept very simple. In all cases I prefer the fixed paternoster, using a small swivel as the junction between hook length and ledger link. Changing down to a lighter hook link and smaller hooks is then both quick and easy. Where considerable weight is required to combat strong currents, bombs are preferable. Otherwise I make up swan shot link ledgers, adding or reducing the number of shots as required, so that the bait only just holds bottom, which is imperative for hitting those slight 'drop-back' indications on the tip when winter chubbing.

Barbel

With barbel bites the rod tip does one of two things, depending whether the fish moves downstream or upstream. Those which grab the bait and move across the swim or head downstream, as most do, result in those classic bites for which barbel are famous. The rod tip simply keels over and keeps going round. Whereas if the fish heads upstream, the tip springs violently back, and sometimes the line can even be seen cutting through the surface, following the fish's direction. That's the nice thing about barbel; they don't hang about.

For close-range swims loose feed is introduced by hand or with a bait dropper, the best attractor by far being stewed hempseed. Maggots and casters either get snapped up by small nuisance fish or washed downstream, whereas hempseed lies on the bottom between the stones as a lasting attractor until the barbel find it. In runs farther out, where it is not possible to hand feed, the block end feeder reigns supreme as both ledger weight and bait dropper.

For the first half-hour or so in a new swim, casts are made at regular intervals, regardless of bites, to build up a carpet of hempseed and hook baits. Anything will work in conjunction with hempseed: luncheon-meat squares, tares, maggots and casters, etc. Worms are great, too, but can prove a liability wherever eels are common. Although considered outdated, sweetcorn is one of the best barbel baits and will score heavily on new stretches where it has not been exhaustively tried. And don't underestimate the power of good old bread. Flake and crust cubes are both effective.

To allow large particles such as corn, small meat cubes, cheese cubes and the like to escape from the block end feeder, simply enlarge a few of the holes with a small pair of scissors. To enable relatively small feeders to hold in fast currents, support the rod tip high, using a telescopic front rod rest which reduces water pressure against the line. Resting the rod butt into the groin should keep the right hand conveniently close for striking, though it is fair to say that most barbel do, in fact, hook themselves, such is the ferocity of the bite.

Care must be taken, therefore, when stepping down to a light hook length. Generally I prefer to use a 5 or 6 lb reel line right the way through to the hook, but there are occasions when, on stretches of river that are heavily match-fished, unless you step down, the barbel simply lie there laughing and refuse to bite. They learn to be very line-shy indeed.

Such was the situation in Series Three of 'Go Fishing' when we visited the lovely little River Teme at Lyndridge in Worcestershire which is permanently pegged and match-fished every Saturday and Sunday by Birmingham Angling Association members. Only when I reduced the 4 ft hook length to 2½ lb test and tied on a size 16 hook holding a maggot and caster cocktail did the bites start coming. They were that shy, despite the river holding a good colour after heavy flooding. It was pretty hairy playing fish of 5 and 6 lbs on light tackle in and around the

submerged willows. But as long as I didn't hurry them, those barbel eventually came to the net and I quite surprised myself in beating them.

To be honest, however, I would much sooner enjoy a real hit and haul tussle of a few minutes on more substantial tackle than a long drawn-out fight. On one occasion I really did wish for a heavier hook link when, just as I was about to net a barbel of perhaps 1½–2 lbs, out of the blue up popped the head of a whopping great pike and grabbed my catch. This commotion occurred in the middle of changing batteries in the camera and before we were ready to roll; whereupon the pike, which looked all of 20 lbs, swam off downstream and promptly bit through the line.

In over thirty years of barbel fishing it remains the only one ever lost to a pike. Wouldn't it just have to happen in the middle of the programme when things were not exactly fast and furious?

During the filming of 'Down on the Avon' Wilson gives a good barbel some 'wellie' to stop it reaching submerged willow branches.

Wading

In the weediest gravel-bottomed rivers such as the Hampshire Avon on the Royalty, our choice for a barbel programme in Series Two of 'Go Fishing', actually wading out into the centre of the river in breast-high waders opens up a whole new choice of swims, most of which cannot possibly be attacked from the bank due to the astonishingly prolific growth of long flowing beds of ranunculus. The barbel occupying the clear runs in between are therefore much more likely to be obliging than those living in all the easily accessible, regularly fished spots.

Provided you fish over a weed bed, keeping it as a sound and sight barrier between the point where you are standing and the run holding the barbel, it is surprising just how close you dare get. In addition to barbel, I took several nice chub and, strangely, for such fast water, a whole bunch of beautiful bronze-coloured bream to around 5 lbs, all on sweetcorn link ledgered. Unfortunately we only had enough time to show a small part of the action in the programme, and the swim was going so well I decided to fish on after the film crew had departed with more than enough in the can. It was just one of those rare days when they wouldn't stop biting.

Chub

Most of my summer chubbing involves carefully stalking overgrown stretches of the River Wensum, freelining lobs and slugs over and between the weed beds or beneath rafts alongside overhanging willows. I catch a lot of summer chub, too, on plugs, so the quiver tip rod does not really get much of an airing until the winter floods have scoured away the infernal blanket weed, caused by the massive over-use of farming phosphates along the entire Wensum Valley. If we are treated to early flooding, I could be chubbing by the end of November. If not, I try to fit in a bunch of sessions from January onwards, regardless of temperatures. In cold weather chub offer just about the most consistent sport, no matter what the conditions, except full spate.

My plan is simple – a large batch of stale bread scraps are soaked overnight in hot water and the excess squeezed out in the morning. I then start at the downstream end of the fishery and put half a dozen egg-sized balls of mash into the head of each likely looking swim as I make my way upstream. Usually I will bait, say, eight to a dozen spots and start fishing at the last baited. Each then has a varying time span for chub to move upstream over the bait before I work my way downstream. It's an effective, lovely way of chub fishing which works especially well on unknown or previously unfished stretches because it provides many of the answers quickly.

As with barbel, end rig is a simple fixed swan shot paternoster with a 3–4 lb hook link and a 5 lb reel line. In very clear water I step down to a 2½ lb hook link and small hooks with maggots or casters, maybe even a small block end feeder. But as a rule a size 10 to a 4 lb hook link holding a pinch of flake or soft cheese paste produces the chub time and time again. The mashed bread never overfeeds the chub because it breaks up into such small particles; thus small balls may be introduced literally all day long. Nevertheless, I always look upon winter quiver tipping on the Wensum as a roving game. It is fun and educational to fish several

The effectiveness of stret pegging is shown in this bag of chub averaging close on 4lbs, all taken on bunches of maggots fished well overdepth in a fast run just three feet out.

different swims in a session, altering tackle accordingly, and then to move on downstream after a fish or three if bites really slow up or stop.

The rod tip is generally positioned high so that the line is not affected by strong currents. Head high is about right, but in strong winds it is best to put up with the flow and angle the tip close to the surface where it is sheltered. In sub-zero temperatures, with a foot of snow covering the fields, a half-inch pull on the tip after a wait of fifteen minutes may often be all you will get; but in mild conditions bites can be real slammers, especially on that first cast into a previously baited swim.

Fishing in this way, I have taken some great hauls from the Wensum, with up to eighteen chub in a session, all from several different swims. The bites to watch out for, which many anglers miss because they do not appear to be bites, are those gentle drop-backs where the quiver tip suddenly eases back a little, long after the swan shot ledger has settled in the swim. You need to be very quick on the strike to hit these, following through in a long sweep back until the hook goes home and all the slack line is taken up. This is because the chub has picked up the bait and moved upstream or across the current instead of heading off downstream.

A lovely slack on the upper reaches of Norfolk's River Yare, simply screaming out to be stret pegged.

Stret-pegging

Wherever barbel and chub occupy deepish runs close into the bank, as they sometimes do beside matts of overhanging sweet reed grass or sedges, I just love to float fish for them. And there is no finer way than stret-pegging, an old-time method which today is sadly neglected by the majority of river anglers. This is a great pity because stret-pegging will catch fish from marginal swims where ledgering creates all sorts of problems, especially bite indication.

With fish which bite delicately or which become scared by the tight line of a ledgered bait, stret-pegging is highly effective because it creates that valuable 'slack' line between rod and hook. Stret-pegging is really 'laying on' in running water with the float attached both top and bottom. A very buoyant float material is required and a 6–7 inch length of peacock quill is perfect – and there you have it – a straight peacock waggler. For fishing at night I simply glue in a 500 microlambert betalight luminous element after first removing with a pin the pith to a depth of 3/16 inch, and then seal with black whipping thread and araldite. The float must be set at least 2–3 ft over depth, and in fast currents this should be doubled, the secret being to encourage a large bow to form in the line between shot and float which greatly reduces water pressure against it. In swims where the current is gentle, pinch on an AA or swan shot at the business end 6 inches from the hook. In faster glides go for a mini ledger made from an inch fold of line holding two swan shots, stopped by an AA shot.

After casting downstream and slightly across, the float should come to rest immediately downstream of the rod tip and lie perfectly flat when the shot has settled the bait. If it tries to cock, push it further up the line. Two rod rests are advisable for this method, so that the angle at which the rod is positioned may be quickly adjusted to allow for current speed against the float.

Bites will be bold, the float simply cocking and slipping straight under, often without any prior warning other than an occasional shake, though such indications, if continual, are the attentions of small fish merely pecking at the bait. During a sensational hour's fishing on the Wensum one blustery October evening in 1984, whilst stret-pegging after dark, using breadflake on a size 8 hook to 6 lb test, I took an unforgettable catch. First came a 10½ lb mirror carp, then a 12¾ lb barbel, followed by a roach of 2 lbs 7 oz, and lastly a chub of 4 lbs 6 oz. When asked what species I was actually fishing for that evening, I usually have to think hard before replying. I had in fact been regularly free baiting the swim every other evening for a couple of weeks with stewed hempseed to tempt a big barbel; and though the Wensum does turn up the odd surprise, this fluke catch went beyond all expectations.

Stret pegging a deep run close beside the marginal sedges whilst the river was up and coloured accounted for this plump 5½lb Wensum chub.

opposite The classic unspoilt habitat of a natural stream in its summer clothes, where dace and grayling hug the gravel runs between beds of streamer weed, while chub and brown trout lie beneath overhangs in wait for the bits brought down by the current.

It certainly illustrates the effectiveness of stret-pegging as a big fish technique, particularly when the river is fining down after a flood and those marginal swims are prime locations.

Whenever the flow is too fast or the swim too deep to ensure accurate free baiting by hand, the use of a bait dropper is invaluable. You can then be certain that both hook and free bait are lying close together.

Stret-pegging also works well during the cold winter months when for chub and big roach I reduce reel line to 3 lb test and hold the rod throughout. Every so often the tip can be lifted and the tackle eased a foot or so down the swim until bites materialise. It's a lovely way to fish.

STRET PEGGING

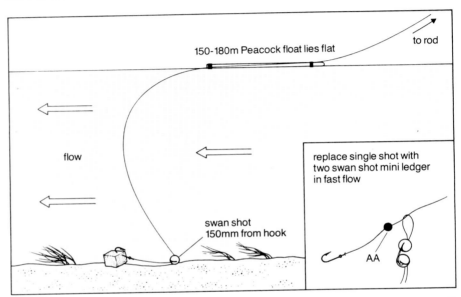

150-180m Peacock float lies flat

to rod

flow

swan shot 150mm from hook

replace single shot with two swan shot mini ledger in fast flow

AA

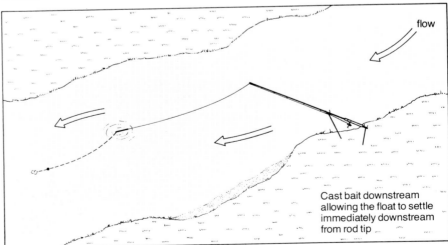

flow

Cast bait downstream allowing the float to settle immediately downstream from rod tip

7
Streams
The Home of Dace and Grayling

It would take a brave man to suggest at which point a brook becomes a stream and when a stream turns into a river. Suffice it to say that my interpretation of a stream is any diminutive, intimate course of flowing water. In origin it might flow directly from rainfall in rocky highlands, seep up through the chalk of Hampshire, or exist as a tributary of a river in the Home Counties. In parts its banks might be so close together that one could almost leap across, yet in other places, especially where it merges with the mother river, or at the junction of other carriers, such confluences could offer considerable width.

By their very nature, streams are rather like children in that they are forever changing while growing, which is why we find exploring them so delightful. As the fluctuating bed of the stream rises from deep, mysterious holes on the bends, and then flows through fast, gravelly shallows, we are drawn downstream from one secluded spot to another in a never-ending search. It is the diversity, the change of character every few yards and around every corner, which encourages the enquiring opportunist fisherman to wander, to alter tackle according to the infinite variety of different swims. Indeed, it is the continual quest for knowledge provided by diminutive watercourses that turns small boys into anglers. At least that's my excuse. I started life as a young fisherman watching the float being taken downstream by the pull of the stream and I have been watching it ever since. Although of course, I have since swapped minnows for larger goals, the stream remains an ecosystem in miniature, with all the features and food chains found in rivers, such as acute bends, glides, gravelly shallows, even waterfalls, hatches and mini weir pools. And it teaches you so much about the life cycle within running water.

Natural history

Simply wading into the shallows and turning over large flints is educational. On the underside will be the tiny cases of aquatic insects which protect their soft, succulent bodies. There will be snails' eggs and algae, rich food for small fishes. Amongst the gravel itself, more creatures, using the flint as shelter, suddenly become obvious once the water clears. Shrimps, probably the most important and prolific food source to most fish in the stream, can be seen scurrying about. Small bottom-dwelling fishes like the stone loach and bullhead also prefer a roof over their heads as protection from chub, trout, perch, grayling and pike, which all too quickly snap them up.

If you look extra carefully beneath large flints, rocks and sunken logs, you might be lucky and see a crayfish. Sadly this freshwater mini-lobster is in fast decline. It does not tolerate pollution easily and in many

Though after dace, John Wilson puts the net under a winter rainbow.

streams has all but disappeared. Where they are still common, however, the very presence of crayfish indicates a pure, clean-running stream with a healthy food chain.

Most stream dwellers eat crayfish. Even dace and grayling will gobble up the ½-inch-long babies as they prepare to leave the mother. At this stage they are little more than a juicy big shrimp anyway. And of course pike, trout and chub will crunch up an adult 3–4 inch crayfish despite its hard shell. A soft crayfish, the name given to the stage at which its skin is still soft after shedding its old shell, is eagerly devoured by everything from dace to barbel. They are immediately aware of its vulnerability, which is one reason why a soft crayfish hides for several days after shedding, until its new rubbery skin hardens into tough shell.

Crayfish share with lizards, slow-worms and crabs the ability to shed an appendage at will, and you sometimes come across an individual with one large and one small pincer, indicating perhaps a previous encounter with a predatory fish.

Lampreys are creatures few anglers ever see. There are in fact three separate species in British fresh water, the largest of which can attain

69

lengths of 4 ft, migrating from the sea into fresh water for spawning, where it lays its eggs in shallow redds amongst the gravel.

The brook lamprey, however, which is the smallest, seldom reaches more than 6 or 7 inches in length and is a regular inhabitant of pure-flowing streams. It, too, hides beneath bottom cover, adhering to stones with its strange circular sucker-type jaws. The infant lampreys, or ammocoetes, which are totally blind, measuring 3–4 inches long and distinctly yellow in colour, may be found in thick silt deposits which form on the inside of acute bends in the stream and immediately behind bridge supports. They feed on nutrients within the silt until their eyes develop and are wonderful natural baits during the 'larval' stage for chub, perch, trout and even grayling.

The most famous of all aquatic insects is the caddis or sedge fly of which there are nearly 200 different species. Affectionately known for the mobile home it builds from particles of stone, sand or wood, it clings to the underside of stones, sunken branches, etc., living a sedentary life. The caddis grub can be carefully removed by simultaneously pinching at the tail end and pulling on its legs from the front. You then have a completely natural bait, slightly larger than a maggot, which can be gathered at no cost whatsoever from the stream itself. As kids we used to collect caddis grubs and catch minnows and sticklebacks on them long before pocket money was spent on commercial maggots. The opportunity is still there for those who take the time and trouble.

Which species?

The two fish species which really flourish and grow to specimen proportions within the limited environment of a stream are dace and grayling. While both may be caught all season through and on a variety of baits and techniques from fly fishing to quivertip ledgering, I love to search for them using the float, and to long-trot, a truly wandering game. It is an exploring, probing, 'I want to know what lies down there' way of fishing, of which I never tire. Quite literally I may walk several miles following a particularly challenging stream, and it's a double pleasure when shared with a good friend. We simply leapfrog around each other trying all the fishy looking spots, sometimes kneeling side by side when a certain glide or pool is large enough to take both floats. Of course, rod hold-alls, heavy tackle bags or seat boxes, rod rests or even a stool play no part in this style of long-trotting, whether summer or winter.

Travelling light

Being hampered with unnecessary items means there is more to clutter about on the bank and make extra noise, and more to hump along when there are miles of tempting swims to search, which can only slow your progress down. Two very good reasons for taking along just rod, landing net and the bait.

Since, as a rule, smallish fish are involved, my preference is for a lightweight, crisp, yet forgiving-actioned 13 ft carbon match rod, together with a centre pin reel holding fresh 2½ lb test line. A selection of floats, hooks and shot are always in my waistcoat which has a large D ring on the back to accommodate a telescopic, folding trout net.

This merely leaves the question of bait, which is carried not in a cumbersome box with a lid but in a two-division bait pouch belted around the waist. Into one side goes a liberal handful of lively brandlings, and the other is half-filled with maggots or casters. As I often return to the car for a lunchtime break when out for a full day's streaming, the bait pouch is topped up again if required. There are lots of other little incidentals in my waistcoat such as a hook-sharpening stone, float wallet, forceps and spring balance, but collectively they weigh very little; and as I use keep nets only on rare occasions, I am free to wander the stream holding just the trotting rod.

A maggot pouch is as much a part of the wandering angler's kit as his rod. Continually opening and closing plastic boxes is both time consuming and unnecessary. Cold on the fingers too.

Summer to autumn

The stream varies little, in physical terms, during the summer and autumn months. Until sharp frosts and floodwater arrive to wash it all away, weed growth generally remains prolific throughout, so you need to be very sure of where each clear run and hole exists. It is a completely different ball game to the long-trotting of winter.

In areas completely choked with weed to the surface, the fish will be packed together in the narrowest of runs and in others spread out all over the place in separate little groups. Dace, especially, fit into the latter category whilst the weed is still up, and so make full use of the inherent buoyancy of casters as bait. A single caster with a size 18 hook buried inside catches up on weed far less than maggots or worms, when the shallowest swims dictate less than 18 inches of line beneath the float.

Well-oxygenated, deepish runs, carved from the bottom by the continual force of water tumbling over into small pools, are bound to attract sizeable shoals. So, too, are those tempting deep, undercut bank runs situated on the outside of an acute bend, particularly if overhung by willows. Because the trees shade the water and restrict light penetration, stopping the weeds from growing, you know there will be a clear run underneath. If the stream holds them, chub and maybe a group of specimen roach will be in residence, with perhaps dace or

71

grayling or both occupying the shallows at the tail of the run well down from the bend.

Very often, the most fishable of summer swims are confluences. Although a collection of silt plus weed beds tends to clog the junction itself where the two flows converge, a long clear run is usually kept open. These junctions are favourite grayling hot-spots, due, I think, to the extra push of water. If you look long and carefully through polaroid glasses, you can even see those grey, shadowy forms hugging the gravel bed. Throw a few maggots into the head of the run and you can actually observe the grayling move forward and snap them up as they sink. The trouble is that maggots, as always, attract trout, which are a real nuisance to the trotting enthusiast in streams stocked for the fly fisherman and which also breed a prolific head of grayling. Rainbows, in particular, are ridiculously aggressive.

Southern chalk streams offer the finest sport with specimen grayling. On a freezing cold day Lee Wilson steadies the net as he draws a River Dever grayling upstream.

No wonder Bruce Vaughan looks pleased, after catching what is a life-long ambition to most anglers. A pound plus dace from Berkshire's River Kennet.

Greedy trout

There is no answer really – no bait guaranteed to interest grayling which the trout ignore. So they must simply be tolerated and handled with care. Remember that they are another angler's sport, so just slip them off the hook without removing them from the water and they will come to no harm. Don't under any circumstances fall to the temptation of a trout supper and pop one down your wellie. Trotting enthusiasts will only continue to enjoy fishing for dace and grayling along streams

73

Concealment and stealth are the hallmarks of the successful stream fisherman. This angler sensibly uses the available cover whilst trotting a bait downstream between the weedy runs.

managed as trout fisheries so long as they respect the privilege. Unfortunately, some greedy fishermen do not and so everyone suffers.

Catching one or two spotties, however, before the grayling get a look in does rather tend to unsettle her ladyship. So if bites are not forthcoming after a hectic, surface-churning battle with a trout, simply rest the swim for half an hour and then return. Such frustration arose on a carrier of the lovely River Kennet in Berkshire whilst filming the programme entitled 'Grayling and the Stream' in Series Two of 'Go Fishing'. I would have preferred to shoot in the winter months when the weeds had vanished and the river held some colour. Trout are then less of a problem, but the camera team had been booked for the beginning of October, so that was that. Quite apart from making fly fishermen froth at the mouth as I walloped out rainbow and browns on maggots, of all things – and from one of the country's most famous chalk streams to boot – those trout were a confounded nuisance.

Even at the end of the trout season, when trotting for grayling is allowed along certain sections of the Kennet, those trout were invariably first to the maggots and far easier to catch than the grayling. In addition, though acrobatic, none of the trout fought any harder than grayling of the same size. So considering the fact that grayling and other coarse species are far more difficult to tempt on the fly than trout, it makes you wonder why trout are put on such a pedestal. I guess it all boils down to finances. There are not many anglers who would be willing to shell out trout fishing prices to catch grayling.

Reading the water

When streaming piece by piece, you gradually learn to expect certain species from particular habitats. That feeling of immense pleasure which comes when the float dips and you hook into exactly what the swim indicated is well justified. The term 'reading the water' sums up the ability of coming to terms with the ever-changing habitat of streams. Get it wrong by walking heavily through soft, peaty banking or walk right up close to where the shoal is situated, and that swim will be instantly 'blown'. Clear-water fish can be unbelievably intolerant. But for those anglers who tread carefully, slowly picking their feet up as they approach the water and then kneel down instead of standing out like a sore thumb, they are readily catchable.

Talking of kneeling, which becomes uncomfortable after a while, particularly if the grass is wet, a ruse of mine may be of interest. I use scissors to cut down a pair of inexpensive, lightweight waders diagonally backwards, starting about 4 inches above the knee. This makes walking as comfortable as in boots, with the valuable addition of a built-in kneeling pad. Try it and see.

Floats and shotting

For the generally shallow situations of stream fishing, I prefer short, squat, trotting floats. The range called 'loafers', being styled in clear

Many fishermen consider brandling worms the best bait for big grayling.

plastic, are particularly suited to shallow clear water and the wide fluorescent tip can be seen at distances of up to 30 yards. Loafers come in five sizes, holding from one to five swan shot, so they cover just about all eventualities. The smallest is perfect for summer streaming, except for turbulent pools, and I fix it to the line with silicon tubing both top and bottom, ignoring the eye in the base. A quick change to another float can then be made without dismantling the rig. In the normally shallow water of streams there is no call for fancy, complicated shotting rigs – not that I ever use them anyway. In turbulent swims, fix most of the shot within a foot of the hook to get the bait down fast and keep it close to the bottom; and in slow swims, bulk most of the shot directly beneath the float with just a single small shot 12 inches above the hook. For deep, slow runs the bulk shot can be moved down to around mid-depth. Keep in close contact with the float tip for striking but not so tightly that it is pulled off course. I find the control of short chunky floats is made easier by slightly overshotting them, thus leaving the merest tip above the surface. I can then even hold back firmly to straighten the line, and lift the bait enticingly upward without deviating from the line of trot.

KEEP SHOTTING
PATTERNS SIMPLE

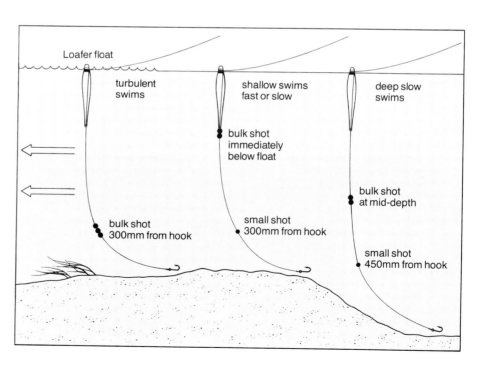

Both dace and grayling respond to the bait wavering upward and then falling again. It may be because that's how loose feed is twirled around

There is quite a difference between male and female grayling. Note the sail-like dorsal fin of the slimmer male (left) compared to the female's noticeably square-cut dorsal.

by currents, or simply because loose feed makes them behave quite differently. Who really knows, except the fish?

The nice thing about summer fishing is that through the clear water you can watch the reactions of both dace and grayling to the way the bait is presented, and then alter accordingly. Laying the bait hard on the bottom is an effective way of catching fish that inhabit short deep runs close into the bank, where the disturbance of continually trotting through and the retrieving of the float directly overhead will easily spook them. Simply pull the float up 3 feet over depth and cast directly into the head of the run – holding back on the float once the bait has settled. It might lie flat or hold in a half-cocked position, depending on depth and current speed. Don't worry either way. Bites will be extremely positive.

Winter trotting

Those who frequent the same streams both summer and winter will already have done their homework by the time the cold season arrives. They will relish the challenge of new areas previously unfishable due to weed, which now provide countless mouth-watering swims. Those long, even-depthed glides are guaranteed to harbour both dace and grayling in quantity, with perhaps the chance of a big roach or two. Confluences will also be full of fish and wherever there is deep, steady

opposite Interpreting
current patterns and
locating the quieter
runs beneath the
surface turbulence is
the secret for
producing weir pool
specimens.

water immediately downstream you could latch on to some of the largest dace.

Males and females

As a very early grouping process to their eventual spawning at the end of March, the larger female dace, pigeon-chested and smooth to the touch, show a distinct liking for the deeper, slower, roachy-looking swims; whereas the smaller wiry males, now covered in minute spawning tubercles and rough to touch, all pack in together along the fastest, shallowest runs. Find one and you could catch dozens and dozens one after another. The contrast between male and female grayling is also very marked but in a different way. The sail-shaped dorsal fin of the male is noticeably very much longer than that of the females, and he is considerably slimmer.

The ardent long-trotting enthusiast knows that the wonderful, most obliging aspect of the grayling is that it will bite positively in the most severe weather. In sub-zero temperatures, when icicles hang from branches which lap turbulent water, when there is ice in the margins and when your fingers feel as though they are going to drop off after just a few casts, grayling bite when nothing else does.

What they dislike, however, is dirty water. I have always found the species loathe to bite during spate conditions. In the southern chalkstreams, so incredibly clear for most of the year, a slightly rising river, with leaves coming down, is enough to put them off. Big dace, roach and chub – no problem. In fact, when my thoughts wander to specimen roach, certain floodwater swims on several streams come immediately to mind, especially quiet lay bays, slacks on the inside of bends and cattle drinks, shallow and unoccupied for most of the year until heavy flooding. Then the roach move in and I catch them by stret pegging with red worms, maggots or casters, after first using the bait dropper to deposit a carpet of loose feed on the bottom. In cold, dirty water roach always prefer a static bait. But even in streams stuffed with them, flood swims do not seem to produce grayling in the same way as they do dace and roach. So give me a crisp sunny winter's day with miles of a little chalk stream ahead, flowing swiftly and holding just a tinge of colour for grayling – and I'll go home happy.

8
The Magic of Weir Pools

I cannot imagine a single more inviting, intriguing and bountiful feature to grace the course of any river than a weir pool – one of my favourite locations. From giant tumble-down weirs on the Severn or Thames to the fascinating little overshoot pools of a meandering stream, weir pools offer such a diverse choice of habitat that numerous species all seem able to live in harmony. They are thus the very heart of flowing water which, due to the high levels of dissolved oxygen, probably contain more fish per cubic foot of water than any other type of habitat along a river's entire course, and are virtually rivers in microcosm.

Weir pools that are still working and flowing strongly are also called mill pools. On the larger rivers without mills, the water level drops down over weir sills through sluice gates, with hand-operated machinery for adjusting the flow rate and height of water in the river above. The weir often takes the main flow of water, whereas the mill pool only opens fully in times of high winter floods, unless it houses milling gear or turbines, in which case it is put to the use for which it was intended. Many rivers have both weir and mill pools situated close together.

When all weirs and mills were under private control, men who loved and cared for the river worked the sluice gates and maintained levels daily. But now, to save on manpower, pressure weirs have been installed in rivers up and down the country. They push excess water quickly through the system. However, when there is little fresh water entering the river, pressure weirs hold it back and so the river below almost dries up, leaving small fish in shallow pools to be decimated by gulls. Quite suddenly, the river rises several feet as the weir gates open and the water above runs off. The gates then close just as quickly when pressure from above is reduced, causing the downstream section to fall again. For both fishing and the survival of small fish upon which the entire river's ecology depends, pressure weirs are a modern nightmare. But enough of the politics – what of the fishing?

Understanding the currents

Many anglers find it difficult to come to terms with weir pools. The combination of the extra push of water, swirling currents and great depths is rather overwhelming, particularly to anglers coming straight from the tranquillity of still water. The recipe for enjoyment and success, however, is to call upon that good old ally 'watercraft'. Start by studying the surface currents carefully for several minutes so as to form a picture of the pool's overall flow pattern. This depends on the direction from which the main flow pours in, and whether one, two, three or more sluices are operative. Some weirs, for example, may incorporate two separate sluices which tumble water into the pool from different

Because fish have to keep on the move against strong currents, weir pools will prove fruitful in the kind of weather when other parts of the river do not.

directions, creating enormous back eddies and subsurface cross currents as the two flows converge.

During the clear water of summer the deeper, fish-holding runs can often be clearly seen, together with all the shallow water weed beds, and even some of the fish. Barbel especially love to lie on the gravel shallows at the very tail end of the pool where they feed on shrimps and other crustaceans plus small fishes. In winter, however, weir pools can look positively hostile, and swirling surface currents do not necessarily portray what really lies down below. But by following the direction of the main body of water you can deduce where the bottom is most likely to be free of weed beds, where it could shelve up and where the greatest depths are situated. Twenty minutes' work with a half-ounce bomb tied to the line will confirm or contradict your suspicions. It will grate and bump over gravel, drag evenly through clean sand, catch momentarily on weed beds, and can be counted down to the bottom to determine the deepest holes. Plummeting will save hours of wasted fishing later on.

The tail end of a pool, where the bottom starts to shelve up both in

81

Go Fishing

OVERVIEW OF
TYPICAL LOCATIONS
FOR PARTICULAR
SPECIES

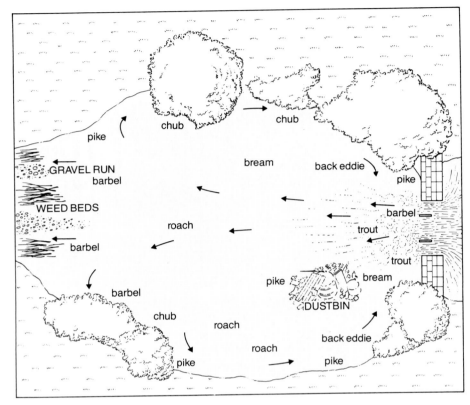

CROSS SECTION OF
TYPICAL WEIR POOL

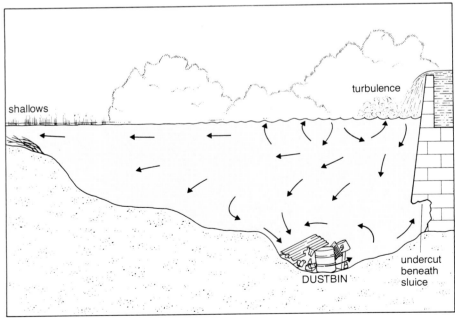

82

summer and winter, is often one of the prime roach spots; and the slow back eddies which form along the sides of the pool could hold more roach and, if there is enough depth, possibly bream. But as no two pools are ever alike you must treat each as an entirely separate entity.

Bankside features often create ideal habitats. Where branches of willows and alders lap the surface chub are bound to be in residence, with barbel beneath them if the run has a gravel or clean sandy bottom and a fair pace. Pike also like lying in such cavernous spots, as do perch or brown trout. Trout love the tumbling, well-oxygenated white water immediately below the sill, where they wait looking upward for small fish disoriented by the currents, and other titbits which the river brings.

River trout are lazy fish, and there is no finer location for latching on to a whopper brownie than in a weir pool. Rarely, however, do they fall to the fly fisherman. The biggest often show only at the tail end of the season when they snap up a small live bait intended for pike. The deepest part of many a pool lies immediately below the main flush where the bottom is eroded by sheer current force. In weirs with one continual wide sill which distributes the water evenly to the level below, depth is uniform, though undercuts form over the years beneath concrete sills, much to the delight of big eels, chub and barbel. But you need a heavy lead to force the bait down fast through the turbulent white water to reach these fish.

Bottle hunting

I have experienced some wonderful, unforgettable moments scuba diving many of the local weir pools of the rivers Wensum, Bure and Yare, in the company of my long-time buddy Sid Johnson. It was Sid who first introduced me to the charm and excitement of 'bottle hunting' - old earthenware jugs, pots, inkwells, marmalade jars, beer bottles and the like. He invariably came up with more of these treasures than I did, my eyes being geared mainly towards fish spotting and the whereabouts of snags in relation to where I normally place the bait. And while this has stood me in very good stead over the seasons, although the character of the bottom does change even from one flood to another, there is a special, personal magic in the discovery of an old earthenware beer bottle which could have been lying on the bottom covered in silt for over fifty years. Several such bottles stare down at me from the kitchen shelf as I sit writing.

Hidden treasure

Sid and I once found much more than bottles when diving the fast

This lovely catch of roach to over 2lbs, chub to 3½lbs and a 6lb bream illustrates the variety of rewards that winter weir pool fishing has to offer.

waters of Hellesdon mill pool on the outskirts of Norwich several years back. To avoid scaring the big roach and chub which always hold on the edge of the main flush close to the tail end of this particular pool, we entered not from the shallows downstream but from the deep back eddy where the bottom was littered with hundreds of old roofing tiles.

Just about everything ends up in weir pools at some time or another, much of it being finally deposited in the deepest, slowest part of the pool. Only eels seem happy to exist in these sterile areas where a motley collection of rubbish and rotting vegetation comes to rest until the winter floods either flush it all downstream or cover it with silt. During the summer, especially, such 'dustbins' are places to avoid.

On this occasion, however, lying among the tiles were hundreds of crimson baize boxes mostly containing rings and necklaces – clearly the discarded spoils of what could only have been a jewellery shop theft. Sid soon had his arms laden with goodies and pointed to the opposite bank where we could inspect our haul. To our disappointment it turned out to be nothing but unsaleable junk, the pearl paint coming off in Sid's hand as he inspected an expensive-looking necklace.

Playing with barbel

By far the most illuminating message that Sid and I have experienced from diving weir pools and many of the stretches in between during the last fifteen years is the way barbel like to communicate with humans. With no other species, unfortunately, does this happen, just barbel. If we approach them slowly they will allow us to cradle them in our arms and even stroke their whiskers. They are incredibly friendly. Much of my time spent breathing compressed air below the surface of the Wensum, listening only to the eerie sound of my own bubbles escaping to the surface from the demand valve, has been passed in the company of barbel, totally fascinated, which is why I have spent more time playing with them than catching them.

Certainly they occupy many of the classic barbel-type haunts where there is a strong push of water over a clean gravel bed. But they also hang out in the most unlikely spots – 'hang' being the operative word. Underneath huge entanglements of sunken branches where the light is very dim I have often come across barbel hanging upside down, completely motionless as if asleep, or with their heads buried among the branches and not necessarily facing the current. In fact, they often hide in deeply reaching undercuts far beneath the bank where the flow is virtually non-existent, a point worth remembering for weir pool fish wherever the banking or sill suggests the presence of undercuts.

Tactics on television

Due to their diversity, beauty and sparkling waters, weir pools are ideal locations for both still and video photography, as indeed was proved by our two 'Go Fishing' programmes which included weir pools. It was great fun, to get my little aquarium net out when filming barbel fishing in the compound weir of the Royalty fishery on the Hampshire Avon, and actually net a few minute barbel. The pool was crammed with fry shoals of numerous species including dace, barbel, chub, roach, minnows, gudgeon plus bullheads, stone loach and migratory flounder. Everything feeds upon everything else in the pool. Chub will eagerly devour baby barbel, whilst barbel like nothing better than a freshly killed minnow, ledgered at the tail end or gently rolled around the gravel bottom where shoals of barbel and chub congregate.

A tumble-over weir on a southern chalkstream which spreads the water evenly across the entire width of the river. Beneath the deep, dark waters live huge grayling, as well as perch, roach and dace of specimen proportions.

Whereas I preferred to long trot the huge, slow back eddy to catch barbel for the benefit of the cameras, presenting a bunch of maggots slowly dragging bottom, I could have caught them with any one of several techniques: rod top ledgering straight down the main flush from the sluices, with an ounce bomb to anchor a fat lobworm or a large cube of luncheon meat down on the bottom; quiver tipping with a buoyant, moving bait like a cube of crust, gently searching across the run and using barely enough shots on the link to hold bottom; stret pegging with float tackle beside the main flush at the end of the slow back eddy right into the bank by the pilings where the bottom quickly shelves to about 10 feet; even trotting down the side of the main flush with a heavy Avon float requiring five swan shots to cock it and baiting with a bunch of casters. That's the beauty of weir pools – they encourage the use of most methods and baits employed elsewhere. And then you may still need to improvise.

Floodwaters

Such was the case when we filmed 'Weir Pool Magic'. Due to the excessive floodwater covering the entire Wensum valley this programme almost assumed an instructional guise, though this was not the intention.

Since the raging weir pool was completely out of the question, I decided to fish where the water had backed up in the normally shallow mill pool, usually just 18 inches deep, but always a good bet under flood conditions. The stark contrast between the completely flooded road and gardens, where even the trunks of apple trees heavy in fruit were now under a foot of muddy brown water, and the scene when we returned to the river once it had dropped within its banks again, would, I thought, provide most interesting television.

In the first part, on that 'flooded day', I managed to catch on casters beneath a waggler about thirty fish from the mill pool in a depth of some 6 feet. It was literally the only spot I could have fished for miles around. The dace, roach and chub which usually live in the main river had obligingly taken refuge in the slack pool to evade the rushing torrent only fifty yards away. Ten days later we returned to film part two of the programme and though the waters had receded, the river still held a good colour with just a little blanket weed coming down. I feel sure this was the reason for such a large concentration of quality fish in the weir pool – fish which under the normal gin-clear conditions of August would possibly have been much further down river.

Ledgered breadflake quickly sorted out some really cracking roach with bites on the quiver tip almost unmissable. In addition to a brace of specimens weighing 2 lbs 8 oz and 2 lbs 9 oz (shown on the programme) – a ridiculous catch for the Wensum in mid-August during the middle of the day – I also took several others up to 1¾ lbs, two 5 lb-plus bream and a 4 lb tench. None of these were included in the programme simply because you cannot cram fish after fish into less than half of hour of television.

A truly memorable catch for John in the 'Go Fishing' episode 'Weir Pool Magic'. Two huge, beautifully coloured roach weighing together just over 5lbs.

opposite John ties a
selection of flies in the
trout episode of 'Go
Fishing' series one. Fly
tying out of doors is
not to be
recommended in a
strong wind!

There has to be time in between each fish to reflect and to include every so often a nature slant – in this case a peep at the eels and a crayfish in the eel trap. There was also a short diversion of my fluking out a nice double-figure pike on a spoon with a little American single-handed bait-casting rod and baby multiplier. In fact, more material ended up in the editing room waste-bin than in the programme itself. The 4 lb tench, incidentally, is only my second ever from the river, and the brace of big roach one of the finest I have ever landed.

I rarely bother with loose feed or groundbait when fishing weir pools during the summer months, as small fish can become rather a problem. So during the programme I ledgered thumbnail-sized pieces of bread-flake on a size 10 hook tied direct to a 3 lb hook link with three swan shots on a fixed paternoster ledger to hold the bait hard on the bottom in the deepest part of the pool: a 12 foot hole where the bottom starts to shelve steeply up, both sides stacked with huge weed beds. The difficulty was to get the bait through the fast turbulent surface water and down to the clean gravel bottom where the roach and bream shoal up.

Inevitably, winter weir pool fishing, with faster turbulent currents, poses extra problems, especially that of loose feeding. To introduce maggots or casters by hand, for instance, could prove suicidal in all but the shallowest and steadiest of runs. The answer is to ledger with a small block-end feeder which calls for accuracy, cast after cast, to concentrate a regular stream of feed along the same line. Otherwise fish will be spread all over the shop. Get it right, however, and there is no finer way of attracting fish to the hook bait. Once water temperature drops to its winter low, a small static bait is far more liable to stimulate interest. So I switch to maggots, two or three on hook sizes 16 or 14 and reduce hook link to 2 lb test.

To stand a chance of hitting the often gentle tremors on the tip of a roach sucking in the bait in cold water, I position the rod on two rests with the tip held high to minimise water pressure upon the line. My striking hand then rests mere inches away. Sometimes I use just the front rod rest and hold the rod with the forefinger of my right hand hooked around the line. It's surprising how even the slightest registration on the tip is also actually 'felt'. During mild spells a lump of flake on a size 12 or 10 hook will sort out the better specimens, roach especially, so the moment small fish start to become a nuisance on maggots, I switch baits.

Whenever a pool can be float-fished through the deep steady water, use a bait dropper to deposit loose feed and fish considerably heavier than the flow would suggest. In fact, to use more weight than less, ensuring at least that the bait is down close to the bottom where the fish are, is a good rule of thumb for fishing weir pools, wherever they are.

9
Modern Trout Fisheries

With so many people living on this tiny island of ours, the pressures on flowing water are enormous. Obviously, not everyone can have his or her own little stretch of river or stream to experience the delight of catching wild brownies. So thank heaven for the rainbow trout and man-made fisheries. Without them there would be far fewer trout anglers around and comparatively few would ever learn to cast a fly and enjoy eating their catch.

Vast deep-water reservoirs unquestionably offer the modern trout fisherman superlative sport because water authorities who control the fishing can afford to stock with thousands of young fish at a time and expect them to grow on in such a rich environment. Furthermore they can feed up others in floating cages at various spots around the reservoir to an instantly catchable size. By comparison, the owner of a smallish stream-fed lake or old gravel working cannot expect to compete. Whereas trout are reared on in many small fisheries to supplement bought-in stocks, unless there is a vast supply of running water close to hand most owners end up spending far more than they envisaged on buying in the larger rainbows which the angler nowadays expects to catch. What is more, due to the selective breeding and feeding of high protein pellets to rainbow trout, which has led to almost mass production of double-figure fish (though at a price), many trout fishermen are no longer satisfied with the possibility of catching 2 lb trout, regardless of their fighting qualities and the surroundings of the fishery. Indeed, in many trout fishing areas around the country, unless fishery owners now stock with a sprinkling of rainbows of over 10 lbs, their business will surely suffer as the floating circus moves on to a fishery which does.

Values and economics

It is a crazy situation and I am sure many professionals associated with modern trout fishing, given the opportunity, would like to reverse this sorry state of affairs. After all, it is not that long ago when the British record for a rainbow trout was just 8½ lbs. And that record from Blagdon, which really meant something, stood for over thirty years

Unfortunately, a similar unhealthy situation exists in modern carp fishing. If a particular lake, no matter how mature, beautiful, secluded or unfished it may be, does not contain carp over 20 lbs, then the majority of carp fishermen are not in the slightest bit interested in even looking at it. It is all very sad.

I highlight these negative aspects, not to knock the out and out 'specimen' or 'trophy' anglers, be they after a double-figure rainbow or a 20 lb carp, but to warn beginners and anyone who contemplates taking

Modern Trout Fisheries

up the art of fly fishing for trout of the possible pitfalls ahead. 'Put and take' trout fishing is a modern invention to satisfy every angler's wish to see a trout crashing around on the end of their line and to feel the excitement of the rod bend as line evaporates from the reel. But it does mean that someone has to put the trout in for you to catch them out, and for this, rightly, you pay a certain price. So there must be a code of ethical conduct if such fisheries are to continue in financial harmony. Owners gear their prices for a day's sport to an average of so many trout being caught, at a certain cost. The difference between that and the price of a day ticket is their profit, once running costs and the rent of the water have been deducted. The trouble is caused by the fishmonger element of greedy anglers who insist on popping trout down their waders in addition to their allowed limit, or who hide away in a corner and throw in handfuls of maggots or sweetcorn, just so that they can say they have taken their limit, while the rest of us are content to observe the fly only rule. The cheats spoil it for all concerned – you, me, the owner

Many modern still-water trout fisheries are born from old sand and gravel workings. With careful landscaping and stocking, exhilarating sport from hard-fighting trout can be had within a very short space of time.

One of John's long time fishing companions, fellow journalist Trevor Houseby, displays a beautiful 5½lb tiger trout. These are stocked into a handful of southern still waters.

and even themselves; for when the fishery is forced to close because it becomes uneconomic, they, like everyone else, have nowhere to fish.

This is why a whole list of do's and dont's appear in black and white on the day ticket. It is a great pity that anglers have to be told not to play their ghetto blaster when fly fishing, not to cast into the stews, not to fish with spinners and not to take home a dozen trout when they have merely paid for the chance of catching four, or whatever the limit for the fishery happens to be.

Being both tackle dealer and angler fortunate enough to own his own fishery, I appreciate all corners of the coin. Into my shop come perplexed and angry fishery owners and managers, describing the crafty dodges their customers employ while supposedly attempting to fool the trout with flies; followed perhaps a few days later by the very same anglers who then tell me how they got away with it. Being in the middle obviously puts me in an invidious situation, although I do treat them to a few home truths, even at the expense of losing future sales.

Early days

I guess one of the reasons why a proportion of today's fly fishermen have no patience with the rules of 'put and take' trouting is because they come straight into the world of fishing from another sport or pastime. Consequently they have nothing in the way of experience or hard-earned values for guidance. I'll never forget those early days with my first fly fishing outfit spent on the upper reaches of Hertfordshire's River Lea. As an enthusiastic young teenager completely new to a world which I had previously imagined to belong only to the very rich or tweed-hatted brigade, I kept plugging away with the traditional method of wet fly fishing. Numerous books had taught me the message of casting the fly downstream and across, and allowing the current to sweep it across the river into my own bank. The only problem was – and I admit to having been terribly naive at the time – that there was no one around to point out that trout in the old Lea were as rare as rocking horse droppings.

So I bumbled merrily on for several years catching dace, roach, chub and even the occasional perch or pike; and my casting into awkward spots improved all the time without my fully realising that I had become quite proficient. Yet because I only ever caught coarse species, I assumed I was doing something wrong. Eventually the penny dropped when I visited a stretch of the nearby River Rib well stocked with trout. Then I came to appreciate that coarse fish are, in fact, much harder than trout to tempt with an artificial.

The thrill of an acrobatic rainbow trout thrashing away on the end of your line is unbeatable. It tastes good too.

The point is, those early informative years of 'apprenticeship' taught me the time value of enjoying fish of all sizes. This is why catching a 2 lb wild trout on a light tackle from an overgrown stream rates just as highly, if not more so, as a prize catch than a stew-fed double caught on heavy gear from a tiny lake into which it was put the day before. Ultimate size is not always the criterion.

With modern still-water trout fishing you must make your own challenges, because it is impossible for the fishery manager to create a stocking policy to suit everyone, or rather everyone's skill level. If he introduces too many trout, experienced fishermen find it far too easy, while the beginners will catch their limits. If he stocks conservatively, ensuring that the expert has an interesting but difficult day to achieve a limit bag, the beginner will probably not catch a thing and thus may not return.

Tactics

It is a typical Catch 22 situation – which is why it is impossible to please everybody. Having driven a fair distance for a day's enjoyment, it is pointless to whack out your limit in a dozen casts on a lure, simply because the fish are easy to catch, for you will be on your way home again posthaste. But by stepping down to a light outfit, fine cast and small imitations, you do have the chance of creating a more interesting day, catching them on dry fly instead of wet, on nymphs instead of heavily leaded lures, etc. This is what it's all about, not catching trout faster than your neighbour.

In the crystal-clear water fisheries of Hampshire, for instance, you may even specialise in stalking the better specimens by casting specifically to individual fish. The most useful outfit for this style of fishing, which at a pinch will cover most eventualities in still-water trouting except large reservoirs, is a 9½ ft carbon rod which takes a size 8 weight forward line. Mine is very light, with a kevlar wrap, and has a crisp yet forgiving action, so necessary for absorbing the lunges of a strong fish hooked in a tight situation. The line I find most versatile is a sink tip, though I suppose I could equally well manage with a floating line and a long cast.

I find so-called 'induced take' fishing a wonderful challenge because success depends upon accurate one-time casting and covering the route of a particular fish, usually with a leaded nymph. Judging the depth at which the trout is swimming through clear water, simul-taneously putting an imitation in its path and then twitching it at just the right moment so that the trout sucks it in is far more difficult than it looks. It is all too easy to misjudge depth in clear water and to think your imitation is on the same horizontal plane as the trout when in fact it is several feet above.

Clear-water fishing also allows you to study the habits of trout and their reactions to various types of artificials. The knowledge gained can then be put to good use when fishing waters where the trout cannot be seen. I can happily plug away all day at a particularly stubborn, crafty trout until I eventually trick it into making a mistake, because deception is the very basis of persuading a fish to suck in a steel hook covered in feathers. The fact that it may only have lived in the lake for twenty-four hours, a week or a month does not bother me one iota, so long as there is a challenge. I know full well, of course, that to take the fly off and put on a fat juicy worm would catch it instantly – just as a machine gun would easily drop a brace of duck or geese. But where, in such cases, is the sense of achievement?

Trouting on the box

Fly fishing for trout is a branch of our sport that I never have enough time for. I relished the thought, therefore, of three consecutive days filming at Bure Valley Lakes near Itteringham in north Norfolk when making the first series of 'Go Fishing'. My good friend and owner, David Green, had generously thrown the place open for us and, as lady luck would have it, even the weather held out throughout the shoot, with plenty of sunshine. More so than any other programme, 'Fishing for Trout' was to include a good variety of natural history, so we required sunshine to illuminate the multitude of wild flowers growing around the lakes and for attempting the tricky job of actually tying an imitative pattern of fly outdoors. Not the easiest of things, especially with a stiff breeze blowing. On more than one occasion the entire trayful of herl, wool, silks and feathers blew away. But we got there in the end, and the pheasant tail fibres that made up the tail of the chosen artificial, a green mayfly nymph, lifted and dropped in a most lifelike manner even when filmed in close-up.

Our main problem was trying to follow a fresh rainbow going at full steam, with the camera and the entire crew needing unlimited patience to obtain any sort of result. Of course no one, least of all the poor cameraman, could predict when it was going to come flying out of the water next. Catching trout for the camera proved to be much harder than expected, despite the liberal stocking policy at Bure Valley. Cussed things are trout; they never take when you most need them to. It was extremely difficult getting through the lesser fish to something which ripped off line and then did a bit of crashing and tail walking. Wide angle shots are always easy, but we wanted some tight shots completely

Variations of the leaded mayfly nymph tied by the author. A firm favourite is the fluorescent lime green pattern, second from the bottom.

filling the screen with jumping trout. Ironically, after spending the best part of an entire day to this end and obtaining nice results, the edited tapes did not cut in too well and were not used in the programme after all. And people ask me, 'John, why does it take so long to make a programme?'

A bygone age

What pleased me about this particular programme – despite its frustrations – was having the chance to show the excavations of a nearly finished pit which, when flooded and stocked as it is now, offers an extra seven acres of fishing, completes the complex of three lakes at Bure Valley and fulfils David Green's lifelong dream of creating a fishery from scratch. Being excavated specifically as a trout fishery, with depths of close to 30 feet, these workings epitomise the importance of gravel pits as tomorrow's fisheries and nature reserves. They will eventually be the only spots to which anglers can retreat in order to avoid pollution, chronic water abstractions, motor cruisers and the like. So, for both trout and coarse fishing in the future, it is essential that we put our eggs into the gravel pit basket now.

The gravel extraction at Itteringham is particularly interesting for its diversity of natural history, being situated within yards of the winding course of the Bure. This is Norfolk's most important and largest river, even though in these high upper reaches, which hold wild brown trout in addition to coarse species, one can wade or even jump across at almost any point. But what has made gravel extraction here so exciting is that deep down in the river valley, beneath the glacial drift, life of the past has been uncovered through many fossil remains dating back hundreds of thousands of years. The site was worked for a period of three years by JCBs for the rich mineral deposits of sand and gravel, but also by diggers from Norfolk's Museums Services, including geologists from Cromer and Norwich Castle Museum, who laboriously sifted through the layers of muds, silts and peats to reveal evidence of bygone ages.

One of the most outstanding finds was the partial skeleton of a woolly mammoth (*Mammuthus primigenius blumebach*) which roamed these lands during the Ipswichian interglacial period over 120,000 years ago. The only remaining sections of the carcass were its pelvis, one complete tusk, a shoulder-blade, several ribs, a kneecap and segments of the spine, suggesting that predators had ripped it apart before it was buried and preserved for all time.

The mammoth and numerous other fossils were preserved in a rich seam of mud laid down during a 10-20,000-year period in which the

Who would fancy casting with this lot underfoot? It's all part of presenting fishing on television.

climate improved after the previous glacial age, allowing woodlands to flourish and warmth-loving animals to return. This seam lay directly beneath the sand and gravel deposits removed by the gravel company; and it also contained fossils of plant and animal species which now survive only in southern Europe, such as the water chestnut, the pond tortoise and the white-toothed shrew, indicating a climate some 2–3°C warmer than exists today.

Scientists suggest that we could now be heading along a similar road because of interference with the ozone layer around our planet. They predict partial melting of the ice-caps which could raise the sea-level by several feet during the next fifty years alone. Not a wonderful thought if you happen to live in Norfolk, one of the lowest-lying areas of land within the British Isles. But perhaps we should look at this continual exchange between land, sea and the elements not in the selfish spell of our own lifetimes but in terms of thousands of years.

The Itteringham deposits also contained the fossils of several identifiable freshwater fish. It is rather encouraging to know that the three-spined stickleback, pike, tench, silver bream, roach, perch and bleak (the last a species not now found in Norfolk, though common elsewhere in south-east England) were all swimming in the River Bure system 120,000 years ago.

opposite
Unprecedented luck during series three of 'Go Fishing'. Working chrome pirks over a wartime wreck lying in 180 feet of water produced these two whoppers. A 17½lb pollack for Roddy Hayes and a 21lb cod for John; his third in two days fishing off Alderney in the Channel Islands.

The future

Wherever pits are being dug with possible future facilities for angling, there should be liaison between all the various wildlife interests and the sand and gravel company long before mineral extraction is completed. Such features as purposely constructed islands for the benefit of wildlife and attractively landscaped banks with marginal sedges and rushes can be planned as the digging progresses, not shoved on as an afterthought.

For instance, wherever the dragline leaves high ridges of undesirable low-quality material or blue clay, which would end up as shallow bars once the pit is flooded, it would take little extra work to convert these bars into islands. The digger/operator could probably utilse poor-quality materials close by, which would otherwise be carted away, for back-filling elsewhere, thus actually saving on excavation time and costs. A small quantity of topsoil over the island and, hey presto, there it is – a feature that adds both beauty and character to any gravel-pit trout fishery, in addition to providing a haven for numerous plants, insects and birds. Islands are particularly useful in small fisheries. Their mere existence creates definite movement areas for trout as well as extra cover from marginal plants and trees. Anglers would always rather look across the surface at trees or rushes on an island, than stare at one another across an open lake.

Islands, and lots of them, are also extremely beneficial in large waters, in that they help break up waves which ultimately cause bank erosion. Long promontories jutting out into the lake are also desirable, not only for the amount of fishing spots and movement areas they provide, but because they, too, help reduce wave action, offering quieter water on the lee side. There is much to do for the future of fisheries, and since most gravel companies really do care about their public image, they are only too pleased, when asked, to help in the planning of future use of the excavations. So it is up to fishermen, among other interested parties, to suggest how best they go about it. The gravel excavations at Itteringham provide just one such success story.

10
'Go Fishing'
at Sea

I have always tried to present programme series with a varied content, but naturally because I live well inland with numerous locations right on my doorstep, freshwater has won hands down over salt. No doubt, if I lived by the sea, as I once did for three glorious years on a beautiful beach in the West Indies, the emphasis of the programmes would be reversed.

I certainly hope the future holds prospects for presenting action in tropical oceans. There are so many exciting sports fish, not found in our waters, to tangle with in the tropics. Which is, I suppose, why I chose the crystal clear blue waters of the Channel Islands for our only sea programme in the first three series of 'Go Fishing'.

Initially I considered the flat beaches along my local Norfolk coastline, and shuddered at the possibility of three days of drizzle and grey skies, or worse still a storm, which, ironically, would ensure a fair catch of cod during daylight hours, but would prove hopeless for filming. And while the best sport is invariably after dark, we cannot film effectively at night, at any rate not for an entire 26-minute programme. Without a background, such material would spell utter monotony.

Furthermore, only a flat calm would permit the cameraman to don chest waders, splash in among the breakers and get another angle by filming back towards the shore. But you rarely catch in flat calms on Norfolk beaches. So I got cold feet and rang my old mate Trevor Housby down in Hampshire, who has sea fished just about everywhere in the world, for an ideal wreck-fishing venue.

Wreck fishing was in fact something I had been wanting to experience for close on twenty years. Few Norfolk skippers specialise in this exciting branch of sea fishing and I never seem to find time for the long drive south-west to Plymouth or Brixham. Trevor suggested the Channel Islands, in particular Alderney, where in addition to deep sea wrecking or bottom fishing, plus trolling for bass, we would have back-up options – in case the weather turned nasty and prohibited off-shore filming – of catching mullet, wrasse, conger, garfish, etc. from the harbour wall or off the rocks.

Much of Alderney's rugged coastline offers superlative in-shore sport all year through and has, in fact, produced no less than six British records: cuckoo wrasse, golden grey mullet, red bream, black bream, blonde ray and sole. My guide Roddy Hayes knows all the local hot-spots and helps each year to organise the local shore festival. I was rather disappointed, therefore, when he rang a few days before our arrival with the bad news that storms had raged for a fortnight, so that in no way could we get out to a deep-water mark. We therefore made alternative plans, even to the extent of possibly filming an hour or two's conger fishing after dark from the harbour wall. Yes – there were

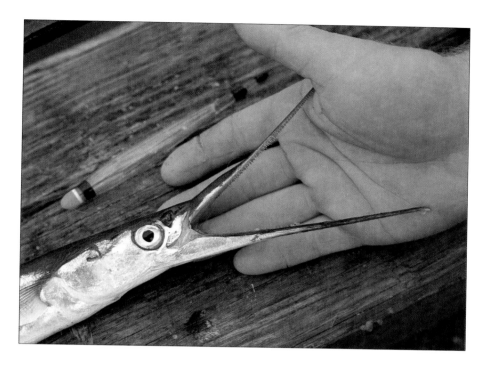

Almost the entire rocky coastline around Alderney offers exciting sport for wrasse, conger, mullet and the strange looking garfish. John caught this fellow from the harbour wall on thin strips of raw steak and simple float gear.

electrical points on the jetty to run the floodlights. Yes – with a bit of luck we could get stuck into a conger. Yes – we could catch species like garfish, mullet and small coalfish in the inner harbour. Roddy must have been sick of all the questions from one extremely worried presenter. I was literally grasping at straws by this time, even to the point of rigging up a wooden frame holding a pair of Optonic electronic bite alarms, fancying that it might be fun to wait for a conger run in the comparatively quiet waters of the harbour – carp style.

I still relish having a go at this because on this occasion it never materialised. The very day we arrived on the island of Alderney the strong gales started to calm. Once again 'Go Fishing' had been unbelievably lucky with the weather. The view from the little Trilander plane as we prepared to land was absolutely breathtaking. Calm, blue, clear seas.

Peter Akehurst and I had arrived one day earlier than the film crew in order to research and arrange things. Suitable boats for wrecking with the Decca navigation system, etc. are limited on the island but Roddy managed to persuade two friends, Mike and Dave, who run a well-equipped 38-footer into locating a particular wreck where good hauls of ling and cod had been taken previously.

Sadly, many of the numerous wartime wrecks lying off the Channel Islands are netted by commercial boats, and the lads feared that this

101

opposite (top)
FISHING ON THE
DRIFT

opposite (below)
There can be few
anglers who would
choose to wreck-fish
for a living. It's arm
breaking work pulling
fish up from great
depths.

previously prolific mark, an old coaster some eleven miles off-shore, lying in 180 feet of water, might have suffered the same fate. The atmosphere on board in the final stages of location was at fever pitch as Dave and Mike used the Decca to synchronise the numbers in Roddy's little black book. And then, quite suddenly, after twenty minutes' quartering back and forth – jubilation. On to the colour screen came the read-out of the wreck below us, which, as the screen portrayed, had not been netted. Hugging the rusted hull were massive shoals of fish, all at various levels according to species. Dave took the boat uptide so that we could fish down its entire length on the drift, and when the hull came up on the screen again down went our baits. We started with a pair of plastic squids on short snoods, the 8/0 hooks baited with strips of fresh sand eel and mackerel caught feathering in just one hour a mile off the island.

Connected to the trace below the baited squids was a two-foot weak link of 15 lb test and a 12 ounce lead. The reel line, being 30 lb test, ensured that the weak line would break first should a hooked fish dive into the wreck and snag the lead. The technique was to lower the baits down until the lead hit the wreck and then come up a few feet, gently easing the rod tip up and down for the plastic squids to attract. Almost instantly we were into them, our first customers being the ever-hungry, goggle-eyed ling varying between 8 and 15 lbs, sometimes coming up two at a time. That's how thickly shoaled they were, interspersed occasionally with the much harder-fighting double-figure cod.

To take the bigger cod Roddy suggested pirks; so once we had filled a couple of fish boxes with ling the squid trace was replaced by a single 16 ounce chromium plated pirk. This was much harder work because to make a piece of steel fixed with a treble hook appear edible you really do need to activate it – physically. First by yanking the rod tip as high and as far back as you can, then by dropping the tip smartly, allowing the bevelled pirk to flutter and jack-knife down to the wreck again, sending out tantalising vibrations. At the end of the drop you repeat the movement. And it is usually just as you start to yank the pirk upward again when a big old cod simply cannot stand this intruder any longer, opens its mouth and grabs hold, almost pulling your shoulders out of their joints.

It really is great stuff. Possibly the most exciting sea fishing around our shores. Physical – yes; primitive – maybe; tiring – definitely. In fact you don't want more than a few hours of hectic pirking, no matter what size the cod run. On this our rehearsal day they ran to over 20 lbs. No sooner had I bagged my first 20-pounder ever, than a second followed on the very next drop. It was fascinating to see these big fish fighting deep down beneath the boat in the brilliant blue void. They looked so

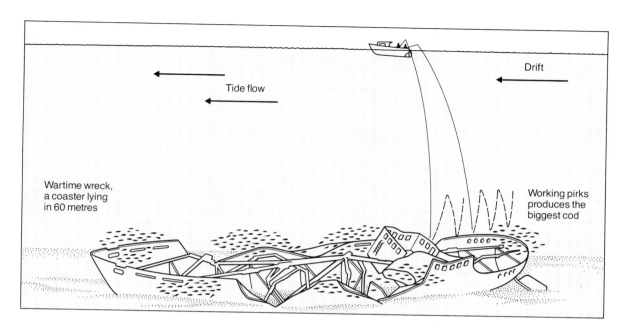

Drift

Tide flow

Wartime wreck,
a coaster lying
in 60 metres

Working pirks
produces the
biggest cod

Big cod go for big pirks. Thinking it's a small fish they grab hold and the treble hook goes home when the rod is worked upwards. Then the fun begins.

In comes a 12lb cod on baited plastic squid. The power of even small cod hooked at great depth is truly awesome.

104

A nice ling ready for the net. Note the coloured plastic squid (called muppets) and 8/0 hooks baited with mackerel.

small, even 30 feet down, but seemed magically to grow to their real size during the last few feet as they broke surface. It was truly wonderful sport and my only regret was that it could not possibly be anywhere near as good on the following day when the camera crew arrived. Yet miraculously it was.

As viewers saw, fishing the same wreck and starting once more with ling, Roddy quickly got stuck into a 17 lb pollack which put up an incredible scrap, and simultaneously I became attached to a 21 lb cod. What a brace of whoppers for the cameras. We couldn't possibly have written a better script if we tried. Roddy's pollack was his largest ever and the best caught off Alderney that year. The main problem now with the programme schedule was our old enemy, time. Bringing big fish up from 180 feet means a long-drawn-out battle; so few fights could be shown in their entirety in the edited down programme, though we finished the day with a bag of over twenty fish. After all, a section of the programme was to be devoted to another slant of Alderney's rich choice of fishing, with me trying for garfish off the harbour wall. By coincidence, too, this was filmed on the same day as the Battle of Britain flyover. Even the Red Arrows were there. Not that we were forewarned, otherwise I might have swotted up on all the planes which flew directly overhead – Lancasters, Spitfires, Hurricanes, etc. My

105

opposite During the Swedish shoot, John takes time to match the wild flowers of the beautiful Klaralven Valley with those in a British reference book.

excuse for not knowing them is that, being a Second World War baby and not a pilot, I spent my youth in the ditches and streams of North London grabbing hold of newts, frogs, toads, grass snakes and the like, while the rest of my class were out plane and train spotting.

Those garfish certainly made me pay for my ignorance. Some days you can't stop them grabbing bait intended for mullet but, try as I might, only on the last knockings did one finally take the float down. Being at the end of the holiday season, I was left trying to catch the fish which had foiled the local kids and tourists. Extremely crafty gars which greedily devoured all the titbits in my shirvy groundbait and left the hook bait. No doubt they had been hooked, pricked, lost, scared or even put back a few times already that summer, so they were as wary as a big roach on a sunny afternoon.

It's funny but we never seem to credit sea fish with the same sense of caution as their freshwater counterparts. The truth is, of course, that whether they live in fresh or salt water fish are creatures which live or die by the rule of 'dog eat dog' - and soon learn. I have caught gars all over the world and never tire of their acrobatic agility on light tackle. I remember once trying to fool them on a fly outfit and small wet flies from Diamond Head Beach in Honolulu many years back. I recollect they were exceedingly choosy on that occasion too.

At the end of the Alderney shoot I had a few hours to spare, though I could have done with a week, so I accepted Roddy's invitation to try rock fishing at a favourite haunt in search of some big mullet he had been keeping tabs on. What do you think we caught one after another? Yes – garfish.

If our trip had been planned, it could not have gone better. The gales had abated and the sun had come out as we arrived, allowing us to film off-shore; and on the day we left a shroud of fog engulfed the island so thickly that the Alderney flights to Heathrow were almost cancelled. Roddy said to me 'Do you realise, Wilson, how lucky you've been?' I did indeed. Our three days were in fact the only, during a changeable weather pattern that persisted for the best part of a month, when we could possibly have put such a wreck fishing programme together. As presenter I am constantly aware that just as easily things could have gone the other way and we would have been able to shoot nothing at all. Being at the mercy of the British weather means that you can only relax when there is enough footage to make a programme. People often say to me – you always look so relaxed, John. If only they knew!

11
Fishermen's Flowers

Fishermen who cannot recognise plants and wild flowers beside the water are missing out on more than knowledge of natural history. In fact, the very spots where certain plants grow are all key pieces in the habitat jigsaw and the secret to putting more fish on the bank. Take, for example, a lake in all its summer splendour: a water rich in marginal sedges, reeds, rushes and overhanging trees, with patches of lilies on the surface. You may never have seen it before, let alone fished it, yet by allowing your eyes to wander from tree to tree and from plant to plant, simply identifying them, you can quickly make an educated guess as to which areas are likely to hold particular species of fish, and even the depth of certain parts. A further hour spent roving the banks and perhaps climbing the odd tree, armed with polaroid glasses and binoculars, could actually provide more information about the lake than might be gained by an angler who has fished it all his life with his eyes shut. There really is no substitute for observation.

Reeds and rushes

Tall marginal plants with spreading rootstocks such as the common reed and reedmace, which sport those large cigar-like seed-heads (often incorrectly called bulrushes), rise up through a few inches to at least 4 feet of water, certainly adequate marginal depth to accommodate even specimen-sized tench, carp, perch and pike, and no further out than a mere underarm flick, even with a freelined bait. Yet so many fishermen destroy their chances of catching such an easy fish by clumping about rather than studying marginal growth. Those who make a point of treading carefully will regularly observe reeds and reedmace 'knocking' as tench feed from the base of the stems, sucking off snails, their eggs and aquatic nymphs.

Marginals which multiply from tubers (in addition to seed, as they all do) such as the beautiful yellow iris and the much less common blue (Siberian) iris, which don't like getting their feet too wet, prefer marshy ground or just a few inches of water. They will tolerate depths of up to 12 inches, however, as will the common fox sedge, easily identified by delicate, dark brown seed-ears.

A similar set of guidelines applies to marginal plants in running water. The true bulrush, for instance, with its dark green onion-like stems, noticeably round in cross-section, prefers to grow in a firm gravel bottom, often in water up to 5 feet deep. For camouflage, perch match the vertical stems with their own stripes while lying in wait ready to ambush a shoal of minnows or gudgeon as they pass. Barbel, too, are never far from bulrushes and love rooting around the base of the stems (you can actually see the stems vibrating even in a strong flow) for

A 27lb leather carp is carefully returned mere feet from where it was hooked; just beyond the marginal covering of amphibious bistort, easily recognisable by the tight, upright, pink flower heads.

aquatic nymphs and shrimps in the gravel. Where bulrushes grow in dense, irregular patches, with enough passages between to conceal pike, a really large fish is on the cards.

Lily beds

Lily beds that grow well out from the bank provide the best visual indication of depth. As they only grow in a water depth of about 1–5 ft, you can be sure that there is shallow water alongside; or, in the case of a gravel pit, that they sprout up from the shallower bars. It is not difficult, then, to imagine where the deeper gullies in between are

109

situated; priceless information when you fish the same pit in winter for pike and the lilies have all died down.

Conversely, for species like carp, it is worth remembering where the lilies provided summer surface shade because carp still frequent the decaying root structure all winter through. In very shallow lakes, especially those of an even depth, old lily beds are invariably the 'hottest' winter swims.

To many anglers, lilies are simply lilies. So in the last programme of Series Two, entitled 'Carp in the Lilies', I decided to don a wet suit and wade into a 4-ft-deep, well-matured lake, 3 ft of which was dark, foul-smelling silt, to illustrate the difference in lily root structure. There is, in fact, a world of difference between the common yellow lily, with its large oval-shaped green pads and those tight yellow flower heads which protrude above the surface sometimes by several inches, and all other varieties of cultivated lilies. Being aware of these facts will aid bait

The enormous root structure and soft cabbage-like sub-surface leaves of the common yellow lily (*Nuphar lutea*).

presentation and help to extract carp and big tench from what appears to be an impenetrable jungle.

The common yellow variety is the only lily to sprout sub-surface leaves, often referred to as 'cabbages'. In slow-moving rivers, where it proliferates along the marginal shelf, the pads and flower stalks often never reach the surface and when they do, boats cut them off. So all anglers ever see are the soft cabbage-type leaves. The big roach of slow-moving rivers can always be located in and around such cabbage patches. River tench love them too. In still waters, carp, tench and bream love to work though cabbages, sucking off snails' eggs and other goodies whilst feeling justifiably safe in the much darkened water beneath the huge canopy of surface pads. Down on the bottom, however, is the immensely thick, turnip-like root structure of this lily. Individual rhizomes can be as thick as a man's leg and a haven to any hooked carp which gets its head underneath. So the point to remember

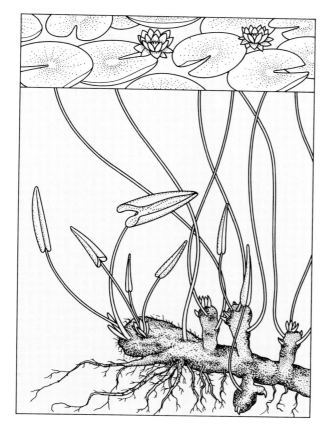

The white 'Alba' lilies and colourful hybrids have a much smaller root stock and a lack of sub-surface leves.

111

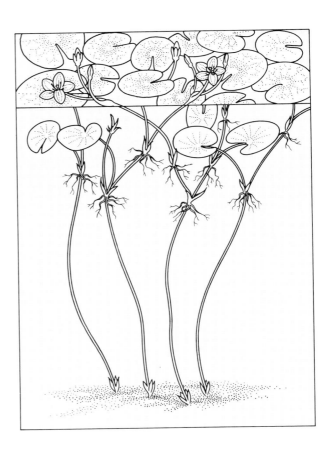

Because of its 'creeping' surface root stock, the dwarf pond lily has far less vegetation below the surface.

when playing big fish such as carp in beds of common yellow lily is to keep the rod tip high up and literally bounce a fish over the pads as you walk backwards. Lower the rod tip to gain line, and down will go the carp into the entanglement of roots and stems. Almost an art form in itself is this technique for lily fishing.

The rootstock of all cultivated, hybridised lilies, from the white albas to the most breathtakingly beautiful reds and pinks, is nowhere in the same league. Neither are there any sub-surface leaves to worry about. Flower stalks and pads, however, are more numerous, so care must still be taken when extracting a big fish. In suitable gaps between pads you can be sure the bait will sink down and show up, whereas it might well rest on top or be totally engulfed by the cabbage leaves of the common yellow lily and thus remain hidden.

Another lily-type plant – though not actually a true lily – much frequented by tench, bream and carp, especially crucian carp, is the

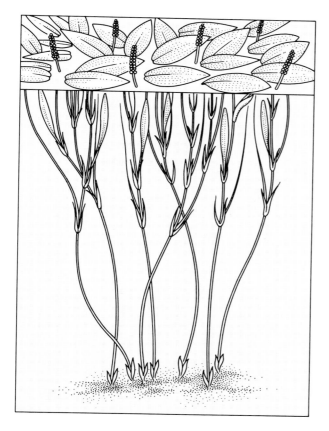

The broadleaved potamogeton has far more vegetation on and just below the surface than further down. Twenty surface leaves can originate from just one stem.

dwarf pond lily, a *nymphoides* species. Its tiny round green pads and buttercup-like yellow flowers form an attractive, if impenetrable, canopy in ponds and lakes where it goes rampant in depths of 2–5 ft. In particularly clear still waters, however, the pads may well reach up through 6 ft to even 8 ft of water – as can the foliage of many lilies if sufficient light penetrates the water.

Because each stalk rising from the bottom may contain several plantlets on the surface, each with its own pads and flower, the sub-surface shrubbery is not that dense. Consequently even large specimens may be carefully extracted without undue hassle – something not apparent from looking at the surface covering.

Oval-leaved surface pond plants such as the broad-leaved potamogeton and amphibious bistort, which are also common in many gravel pits, provide great hideouts for carp, tench, bream and particularly perch. Both have pinkish, knotty seed-heads held above the

113

surface on straight stalks and both have little in the way of sub-surface greenery to hamper the playing of a good carp on substantial tackle. And that's the nice thing about fishing deep among plant jungles. Since the line is nowhere near so apparent, you can increase tackle strength accordingly without spoiling bait presentation.

A splash of colour

The species of wild flowers found beside the water are far too many to list here. Some are both fragrant and colourful, like the family of water mints which sport purple flowers. Over the years 'crushed water mint' has rightly become synonymous with early morning tench fishing. There is no finer smell to greet the early riser. Some plants purely provide a mass of splendid colour, like the pink and white flowers and crimson red stalks of the Himalayan balsam or 'jumping jack', as it is better known, for the way in which the seeds are catapulted from the pods by internal springs. It colonises and beautifies river valleys in many counties.

The flowers of Himalayan balsam come in both pink and off-white, while the stalks are rich red. The seeds are spread by a catapult mechanism which accounts for its popular name 'Jumping Jack'.

Some plants provide colour when there is precious little else around, like the buttercup-yellow blooms of the marsh marigold, one of the earliest marginals to flower. Others radiate beauty at the end of the summer, notably the pink mass of the rosebay willow herb. This particular flower, long my favourite, is now almost synonymous with 'Go Fishing'. Friends tell me that by hook or by crook I manage to introduce willow herb in almost every programme. This is not strictly true, but I probably mention it more than most wild flowers simply because it colonises the banks of so many fisheries, from streams to gravel pits, providing tall cover and a maze of colour from July right through until the end of September.

Even when 'Go Fishing' visited the county of Varmland in Sweden, what was the most common wild flower? Yes – willow herb. The great or hairy willow herb is pretty, too, with numerous single flowers to each stem as opposed to the lupin-like mantle of the rosebay.

Basically there seem to be two distinct colour ranges dominating wild flowers by the waterside: yellow and pink-mauve. Many of the plants, including those already mentioned, have yellow flowers, as do some of the shrubs like gorse and broom. Complementing the pink range are the centauries, campions, purple loosestrife and the foxglove (which also comes in white), to name but a few.

Without this splash of colour our fishing world would just not be the same. To fish and catch nothing amid a patch of colour and scent is more enjoyable than blanking on the local canal or city river between concrete banks. It's part of getting away from it all; a well-worn phrase

but one that needs repeating every so often. I know many fishermen who take the time to gather the seeds of their favourite wild flowers in order to scatter them beside fisheries wherever they go. Indeed, isn't this how fish themselves have been spread about? Contrary to River Authority rules, perhaps, but we can't always rely on River Authorities to provide our fishing, can we? I well remember Old Albert, a brickie's labourer, who worked with my dad on a large building site in Chingford when I was a kid. Albert had kindly given me six young crucian carp for my fish tank which he caught from a tiny pond on the outskirts of Epping Forest. Many years later dad told me how, after a hard day's work on the site, Albert would bike the ten miles to his crucian pond for an hour's fishing and afterwards transfer his catch from an old bucket dangled across the handlebars to all the ponds in Epping Forest. I like to think there's a bit of 'Albert' in all fishermen.

Amongst a profusion of wild flowers and water lilies young Oliver Collins lovingly cradles the result of the programme in series three of 'Go Fishing', entitled 'Ollie's First Carp'.

Conservation and the lead shot issue

On a very personal level, one of the most rewarding aspects of our programmes was being able to interview Len Baker of the Swan Rescue

Foxgloves are so beautiful and of such intricate design, they might easily compete with cultivated varieties at any flower show. But here they grow wild and self-seed, flourishing in soil which is sandy, stony or loamy.

Service and finally to put the lead shot and swan deaths debate into perspective. Fishing has been very good to me and so it was nice to put something back. I have always believed that we anglers can only look forward to the future if we recognise and try to understand the problems facing creatures who share the waterside environment.

Since Swan Rescue was set up in 1977, angling has taken a lot of stick over the lead shot issue, and an interview with the 'arch enemy' could have been deemed almost suicidal. But I knew Len Baker better. During the chubbing programme along the River Wensum, our lengthy discussions involved some straight talking – the dialogue was uncut – and we looked at what were then 'new lead-free substitutes'. It all did more good than harm. I have certainly learnt a good deal more about the plight of swans and other water birds by talking with Swan Rescue, and I like to believe that as a result I am more responsible for my actions.

For many years we anglers tried to sweep the lead shot problem

Fishermen's Flowers

under the carpet and pretend it didn't exist. Some even thought it would blow over without our response. The media, as usual, misrepresented both sides of the argument and so the division widened. I even heard so-called experienced and responsible anglers, including club officials, say that because they had personally never seen a dead swan it was all a load of old rubbish. Talk about putting your head in the sand.

To be fair, Swan Rescue have always insisted that anglers' lead is only part of the massive problem facing many species of water birds. Overhead power cables, for instance, are responsible for almost as many deaths as angling split shot, whilst the lead from wild fowlers' cartridges also contributes, especially to the deaths of whooper and Bewick swans. Wherever clay pigeon shooting ranges border on to water, river or lake, the enormous build-up of lead shot poses a particular threat to swans. As with fishing split shot, cartridge shot is picked up by the birds and taken back to the gizzard where it is used as a grinding agent to break down vegetable matter. Brutal vandalism from

A profusion of yellow from one of nature's most prolific and energetic self-seeding plants; the evergreen broom, whose seed pods can be heard cracking open in hot weather as the seeds are scattered.

117

It's not difficult to understand why swans are so photogenic. John's involvement with the Swan Rescue Service, based near Norwich, and the lead shot issue, were brought together in series one of 'Go Fishing' in the chubbing episode along the River Wensum.

hooligans and injuries caused by boat propellers also come high on the fatality list.

One of the biggest problems in Norfolk's tidal waterways is the commercialisation of the Broads and the escalating hordes of motor boats which have robbed the waters of soft weed and destroyed the natural balance of habitat. So instead of consuming their natural diet of soft weeds, swans grub about in the bottom silt for algae foods and thus pick up discarded lead shot and end tackles. Summer traffic also attracts 'holiday fishermen' whose only claim to angling fame is the purchase of a toy fishing outfit during their weekly cruise. Many show neither care nor sense and many a true angler takes the blame for their activities.

I remember Len Baker ringing me on a Sunday evening, 14 June 1987, two days before the coarse fishing season was due to start. Tired and extremely upset, he had just returned from recovering the bodies of four dead swans on Hickling Broad and counted no less than forty-two people fishing. Need I say more?

Our obligation as anglers

Really there are times when as an angler I feel truly ashamed of my sport. Ashamed of being linked with those who litter the banksides because they are just too lazy to take their rubbish home; who leave tackle caught in a tree without even attempting to retrieve it; and who rip

Dick Brigham and his colourful hen buzzard 'Spectre' made a wonderful diversion in the 'Search for a Trout' episode of 'Go Fishing' series three.

opposite Depending
on how they are
arranged, fish make
interesting subjects,
even just their heads.

line from their reels and thoughtlessly, uncaringly, throw it away, when it is so easily made harmless to wild life by cutting into short pieces with a pair of scissors or simply by striking a match. We have partially put our house in order by switching to non-toxic substitutes, since the sale of lead split shot from size 6 up to 1 ounce bombs was banned in the UK in January 1987. But it would be nice to keep the name of angling clean by reminding ourselves continually of our obligation to the environment, to leave our patch of the bank as we found it – not so much for fellow humans who use the water as for the animals whose claim to it is incomparably greater than our own.

There is a very pleasing postscript to this issue. Known for being as quick to praise as he is to condemn, Len Baker rang me early in October 1988 with some wonderful news. From June 1988 Swan Rescue had recorded 155 fewer deaths from lead poisoning than in the previous year, resulting in a 61.75 per cent drop. These official findings were only for the Anglia region and in the Thames area figures were even lower. Everyone assumed, even when we switched over to non-toxic split shot, that the lead already lying on the bottom would continue to be responsible for swan deaths for many years to come, and in some cases this may still be true; but in most fisheries the old lead shots are sinking deeper into the bottom silt (and beyond the reach of swans) more quickly than expected, resulting in far fewer deaths. A most encouraging reward for all parties involved. Well done, Len.

Had there been more time, I would have liked to include very much more wildlife, particularly birds, in our 'Go Fishing' programmes. But as we never use any library stock, only the material taken on location during each three-day shoot, time nearly always wins. I was particularly pleased, therefore, to introduce my good friend, Dick Brigham, his lovely hen buzzard, Spectre, and his unusual collection of diving ducks in our 'In Search of Trout' programme filmed along my local Wensum Valley. We were initially worried that Spectre would be too ill for the programme as she was rather poorly for several weeks prior to shooting. And although she performed admirably and gracefully on the day, our fears were well founded. Sadly, Spectre died a few months afterwards, leaving Dick heartbroken.

12
Fishing in Focus

My first fishing camera – indeed my first camera – was Dad's old box brownie purchased before the Second World War. Because of its large 127 negative size, it produced passable black-and-white photos. Passable, that is, for that period. Unfortunately I dropped it in the mud beside the River Lea when barbel fishing one Sunday morning. After that, looking though the view finder was never quite the same. There followed numerous plastic bodied, built-in flash specials, none of which lasted more than a season, and then an all-metal 35 mm camera.

An interest in colour slides soon developed when I was given a projector for a birthday present, as well as a desire to obtain good fishing photos. I got immense enjoyment from giving 35 mm slide shows to the local fishing club and spent all my spare funds on film.

Although artistic efforts during my teens seemed largely wasted due to the number of wrong exposures, bad compositions, etc., it was nonetheless a valuable apprenticeship, providing lots of experience in the field; and for that there is no short cut. Overall, exposure was the biggest single problem in those days of hand held meters and guesswork, so many shots being either too dark or too light. Thanks to the modern technology built into even the cheapest cameras, this is largely a thing of the past; but I often think that anglers would nowadays take far better photos had they first experienced the problems of completely manual cameras. At sunrise or even at sunset, for example, when there is never as much light about as you think, experience and a host of past failures will signal a warning, and so you compensate by overriding suggested exposure by one or two *f* stops. Or you will reset the film speed collar to 50 or 25 ASA when, for instance, you are using 100 ASA film, simply because the automatic exposure is lying and you must respond accordingly.

The secret, of course, is knowing when. Fortunately, with most modern automatic exposure cameras, there is absolutely no need to 'bracket' or alter the auto setting during normal daylight conditions, whether dull or sunny.

Shutter speeds

Because many fishing photographs, particularly of large specimens being caught, are taken during fairly low light conditions, you must ensure that the shutter opens and closes fast enough to capture action shots and to alleviate camera shake. You need a minimum shutter speed of 1/125 sec., for instance, to freeze the action of someone playing a fish. Anything less and the vibrating rod and hand movements could be blurred. To freeze a fish swirling as it nears the net or the fish actually in the net, being lifted out, go for a minimum of 1/250 sec. And

Use a shutter speed of 1/500, or better still, 1/1000 of a second if you wish to freeze water and the action, as in this shot.

for tail-walking pike or trout, 1/500 sec. or better still 1/1000 sec. is required if you want really 'frozen' results with suspended water droplets in mid-air, etc.

The snag is that whenever shutter speed is increased, the lens must be opened wider to let in sufficient light during a shorter space of time. This means a large aperture, and stops down to $f/2.8$ or less, resulting in a much reduced depth of field. So you must be extra careful to ensure that everything you want is properly in focus.

Depth of field

For maximum brightness, all single lens reflex cameras are designed so that you view through the lens with the iris wide open. It only closes down to the desired f stop when you actually press the shutter. Some cameras have a depth of field preview button which momentarily closes

1. SMALLER
APERTURES
PROVIDE A GREATER
DEPTH OF FIELD

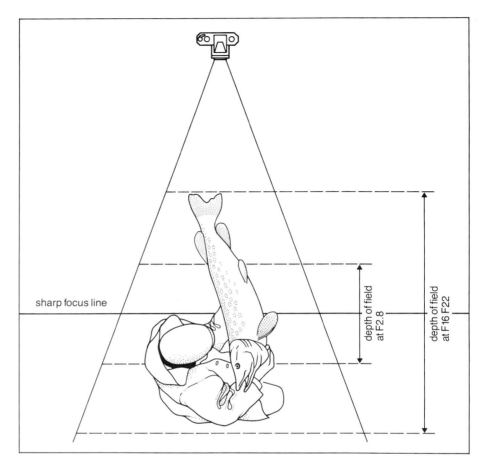

sharp focus line

depth of field
at F2.8

depth of field
at F16 F22

the iris down so that you can see what is going to be in focus and what is not. For cameras which haven't, you must be careful in low light values when shooting with the lens wide open. Conversely, when it is closed down to apertures such as f/16 or f/22, you enjoy maximum depth of field (Diagram 1).

Where the depth of field is going to be minimal, and you want a trophy shot, it is best for the angler to position himself side-on to the camera and hold the fish out so that it too is side on, exactly the same distance away from the lens (Diagram 2). Both subjects will then be in equally sharp focus. If the fish is held at arm's length well in front of the angler, one or other is bound to be out of focus (Diagram 3).

Depth of field decreases, of course, when the focal length of the lens is increased. This is why a telephoto lens is great for capturing the subject alone in sharp focus (i.e. the angler holding his fish) with everything in the background unrecognisably out of focus. At the other

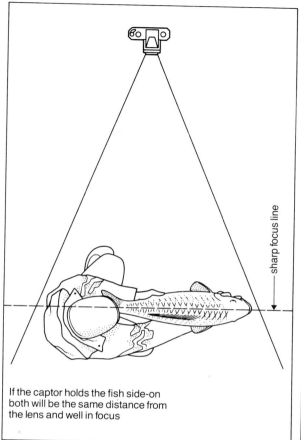

If the captor holds the fish side-on both will be the same distance from the lens and well in focus

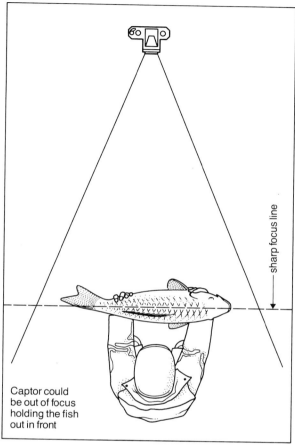

Captor could be out of focus holding the fish out in front

end of the scale, wide-angle lenses have an enormous depth of field, so it is possible to have everything in focus from just a few feet away to infinity. This is why all basic cameras are fitted with a wide-angle lens.

To ensure good action shots with a fair depth of field – stops, say, between $f/5.6$ $f/8$ – sunny conditions are imperative. Alternatively, you can cheat the weather by using a fast film with a rating of 400 ASA, or even 1000 ASA instead of the normal 100 ASA, which allow fast shutter speeds to be used in conjunction with suitable apertures. Fast films simply accept what little light exists much more quickly than normal-speed films. You pay for it, however, with less definition and colours which are nowhere near so bright and crisp. With action photographs it is always a case of compromise, but well worth the effort. Good photos rarely just happen; they are the result of planning and a carefully adjusted camera held in steady, experienced hands, no matter what trendy camera adverts tell you.

2. & 3. IN LOW LIGHT CONDITIONS ESPECIALLY, SHARP PHOTOGRAPHS DEPEND ON HOW THE FISH IS HELD.

125

John's brother, David Wilson, cradles a bream to the side, maximising on depth of field, and ensuring that both fish and captor are in sharp focus. The worm dangling from the fish's mouth helps to tell part of the story.

Framing

Merely to press the shutter, having set at a suitable speed commensurate with an ideal aperture, is not the slightest use, of course, if you haven't thought about framing the subject in the first place. We have all endured those perfectly exposed shots of a fish with its head or tail missing, the angler with his smiling face cut in half, the telegraph pole poking through the top of his head, or the subject forming such a tiny portion of the frame that it's hardly worth the trouble of having a print made. Good for a laugh, but not much else.

Framing is probably the single biggest mistake made by all who wield a camera, not just anglers. The secret is to think seriously about what you actually wish to capture on film and then plan accordingly. For instance, if there is a huge great carp or pike in the sack awaiting a trophy shot, don't let it flap around on the ground while you work out the best angles and light conditions. Plan it all beforehand. A shot with a background of a field full of grass is idiotic. Instead, get the captor to take up a natural position alongside the water, or even to wade in, where wild flowers, reeds or rushes can be included to enrich the finished product. Then ask him to hold his hands up palms facing the camera, moving them slowly to the left and right until the light catches them evenly. Remember that – evenly. Shadows ruin so many potentially good trophy shots. Then, and only then, should the sack or net be lifted from the water and the fish photographed with the minimal amount of trouble. Provided light conditions are favourable, the very best time to photograph a sizeable fish is immediately after it has been caught when it is still exhausted. After a good rest in a net or sack, it may liven up to such an extent that it becomes almost impossible to hold. So if you want a trophy shot, take it straight away. Simply leave the fish in the landing net in the margins, without even bothering to take the hook out, and work out the shots you want.

If a friend is at hand, rehearse the positions required for correct framing. The fish will come to no harm lying quietly in the net. Then you can easily capture an action shot of lifting the net out, unhooking the fish with forceps, or simply displaying the trophy. And finally, even one of weighing or returning your catch. My tip is to unscrew the landing net and frame and hook it complete with fish on to the scales (deduct its weight afterwards) instead of using a separate weigh net or sling. Then all the important shots will be recorded without putting the fish through any more rigmarole than is necessary. It is easier for you and certainly much better for the fish than to keep shoving it in and out of nets and sacks – believe me.

Filling the viewfinder

Whether you are after action, close-up or trophy shots, always try to fill the viewfinder with the subject. On the large format cameras used by professionals, with bigger negative or transparency size, it is sometimes an advantage to leave a gap at the side or at the top for editors to crop or include a title. But for fishing snaps get used to *filling* the frame. There are no prizes for half field or river, and half angler with fish.

Don't simply photograph the fish lying on the grass by itself without a guide to its size. Take off your watch, use a flower or two, a pair of forceps, anything that relates in size and perhaps adds a splash of colour to the close-up. Bags of fish invariably look messy, especially when they jump about and become covered with grass or leaves. Far better to capture a bag of roach or bream still in the net (shake the net so that the mesh doesn't trap water), or show a brace or an individual fish nicely held by smiling captor. Looking at pictures of miserable anglers proudly holding 'big fish' is worse than watching paint dry. So joke with your subject, tell a funny story, swear, tell him his rod has just been pulled in, anything to prompt a reaction. The resulting photo will look so much better. It's old hat, but simply saying 'cheese' still produces the goods.

After several years of fish photography you will no doubt be looking for those odd, unusual shots which capture the essence of fishing in a

As anglers love to fish on into darkness when the weather permits, the option of capturing stunning sunsets, like this shot, occurs frequently.

slightly different way. It could be a beautifully moody, frosty or snow scene, the close-up of a fish's jaw structure or its scale pattern, and so forth. There really is no end to the permutations; only your mind will limit the diversity. Landscapes that include a river valley or lake, for instance, invariably look more interesting when framed with the tips of bushes, grasses or trees in the foreground. To capture still-life shots of small fish like perch, dace and grayling, include your reel and float wallet or bait, etc. Pick some berries, colourful leaves or old bark from fallen trees. Props add interest and colour to the smallest of fishes. It pays to experiment, otherwise you inevitably end up with a motley collection of prints or transparencies, 90 per cent of which are trophy shots.

For my own photography I have two systems. One is of medium format, a Bronica ETRS which takes 120 roll film and produces fifteen 6 x 4.5 frames, double the image size of 35 mm. Although bulky, heavy and rather cumbersome, some editors prefer the larger image size because it is capable of being cropped and of course blows up extremely sharp. Yet nowadays the reproduction on 35 mm negative and transparency films is so good, I often wonder if I am not simply kidding myself that the larger format is better.

In addition to the standard Bronica lens, I have a 200 mm telephoto and a wide angle, plus a pistol grip handle with built in lever wind which makes the ETRS almost as fast as a 35 mm camera. It has removable backs, each with its own dark slide, allowing me to swap from fast to slow film, from black and white to colour, or from negative to transparency. I must confess, however, that in recent years I have used 100 ASA Fuji transparency film almost exclusively. The colours seem to suit fishing perfectly. Lugging the Bronica outfit along on every trip (it actually weighs 15 lbs) is just not on, so for lightness plus versatility in 35 mm photography I use a Nikon 301 with a 35 mm to 105 mm telephoto lens. With a built-in motor drive, auto exposure and

There are countless ways of composing still life fishing photos without so much as a fin in sight. This selection of colourful lures displayed on a pile of cut logs contains both contrast and interest.

When planning a still life close-up of a trophy fish, try to include the colour of wild flowers in the composition.

shutter speeds to 1/2000 sec., this little workhorse covers just about all my fishing requirements except extreme telephoto work.

The 35 mm–105 mm tele lens is versatile enough to capture anything ranging from wide-angle shots, if out boat fishing for pike, to trophy shots with the background completely frozen out. With built-in macro facility, this lens also enables me to fill the screen with a 4-inch roach. So it really does cover most situations. There are times when I could do with a wider angle, say down to 28 mm or even 20 mm for those extremely tight situations, but I am willing to compromise with just one lens for the freedom of carrying less equipment around in the course of roving sessions.

Filters

An inexpensive way of capturing close-ups with your camera's standard lens is to invest in a couple of diopter close-up lenses. A 1x and a 2x, for instance, may be used singly or together for a 3x magnification. A polarising filter is extremely useful for filming plants or fish beneath clear water, or for reducing glare when photographing a particularly reflective surface. I must admit to being rather unadventurous with colour filters, though I do insist on having a skylight 1A screwed into each lens, not so much for its intended purpose of cutting out ultraviolet

The old saying 'the camera never lies' is not strictly true. Without a polaroid filter there is nothing to see.

Screw a polarising filter into the front of the camera lens and the swim actually contains a trio of feeding carp.

rays as for lens protection. I can then continue my bad habits of cleaning the filter glass with anything that comes to hand, handkerchief, shirt-tail, etc., instead of a proper lens tissue. In the event of scratches, all I have to replace every few years is an inexpensive filter glass instead of the lens itself.

So far I have purposefully omitted any reference to the use of flash in fishing photography because in this limited space and given the variety of modern flash set-ups, there is no way of doing the subject justice. Fortunately, many 35 mm camera systems now come fitted either with built-in flash or with dedicated flash facilities which eradicate much of the hassle in photographing, say, the highly reflective scales of a fish, particularly of silver-sided species such as roach and dace. Even with dedicated flash, however, where a micro-computer works out the correct exposure and flash strength, I remain sceptical, particularly with special, one-off, unrepeatable catches. So I still tend to 'bracket' just to be on the safe side by also taking the shot one stop either side of the camera's auto choice. Then I can sleep easily.

Self photography

On the programme entitled 'Carp in the Lilies', the last in Series Two of 'Go Fishing', I mentioned how easy it is actually to take your own trophy shots. A simple bank-stick camera adaptor and a cable release which screws into the shutter, worked by an air bulb on which you tread or kneel, are all that is required. The total cost is less than the price of two rolls of film, and for the angler like myself who regularly fishes alone, it is absolutely invaluable. What I failed to illustrate, however, due to the lack of time, was how easy it is to photograph yourself in action. For this a wide angle lens is preferable, due to its greater depth of field and obvious wide angle of view. With a standard lens the camera needs to be much further away to get everything in, and you would require a long cable release, but a standard lens will do at a pinch. The secret once you are catching fish is to take a few minutes off to set it all up. Start by positioning the camera to your left or right, whichever allows a full view of you side-on. Use a long telescopic bank-stick so that the camera is at least 3 feet off the ground.

Ideally, the sun should be coming from behind the camera or the scene nicely illuminated if overcast. Set the focus, aperture and shutter speed accordingly and then screw in the shutter release, trailing the cable around the outside of the frame so that the bulb can be operated by the foot further from the camera. If sitting, ensure that the stool appears in the very edge of the frame, allowing a wide view to get the rod in when playing or landing a fish (Diagram 4). And that's about it,

Fishing in Focus

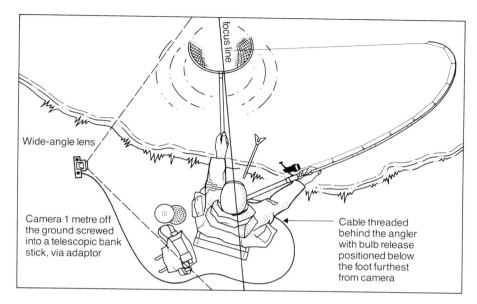

focus line

Wide-angle lens

Camera 1 metre off the ground screwed into a telescopic bank stick, via adaptor

Cable threaded behind the angler with bulb release positioned below the foot furthest from camera

really, except to make sure the cable is well hidden. In soft ground I rest the air bulb on a small plastic box so that the shutter fires instantly to the slightest foot pressure. I can then capture exactly what I want: playing a fish when it swirls on the surface, netting, lifting the net out, or whatever.

Cameras which have built-in motor drives and accept a push-button cable release enable you to take an entire sequence of shots without having to rewind between each. Otherwise you can only take one frame before needing to wind the film on. So make the very best of the action. At least with self photography you have only yourself to blame.

Good fishing!

JOHN WILSON

133

Index